Participatory Culture in a

Participatory Culture in a Networked Era

A Conversation on Youth, Learning, Commerce, and Politics

Henry Jenkins, Mizuko Ito, and danah boyd

polity

The right of Henry Jenkins, Mizuko Ito, and danah boyd to be identified as Authors of this Work has been asserted in accordance with the UK Copyright, Designs and Patents Act 1988.

First published in 2016 by Polity Press

Polity Press
65 Bridge Street
Cambridge CB2 1UR, UK

Polity Press
350 Main Street
Malden, MA 02148, USA

ISBN-13: 978-0-7456-6070-7
ISBN-13: 978-0-7456-6071-4 (pb)

A catalogue record for this book is available from the British Library.

Library of Congress Cataloging-in-Publication Data
Jenkins, Henry.
 Participatory culture in a networked era : a conversation on youth, learning, commerce, and politics / Henry Jenkins, Mizuko Ito, danah boyd.
     pages cm
 Includes bibliographical references and index.
 ISBN 978-0-7456-6070-7 (hardback : alk. paper) -- ISBN 978-0-7456-6071-4 (pbk. : alk. paper)
 1. Internet and youth. 2. Online social networks. 3. Technology and youth. 4. Youth--Social life and customs. 5. Youth--Political activity. I. Ito, Mizuko. II. boyd, danah, 1977- III. Title.
 HQ799.9.I58J46 2015
 004.67ʾ80835--dc23
                                                                    2015012712

Typeset in 10 on 14pt Utopia by
Servis Filmsetting Ltd, Stockport, Cheshire
Printed and bound in the USA by Courier Digital Solutions, North Chelmsford, MA

For further information on Polity, visit our website: politybooks.com

Contents

Preface

Anonymous, 4chan, Harry Potter Alliance, *Kony 2012*, Facebook, Instagram, Minecraft. In the twenty years since Henry Jenkins first began talking about what he termed "participatory culture," the concept – and the term itself – has gained wide traction across a range of disciplines as scholars have sought to respond both to new cultural practices and to the new affordances enabled by digital, networked, and mobile technologies. And, not surprisingly, participatory culture as a concept has also come under sharp criticism and even attack from some quarters. The goal of this book is to critically examine the concept of "participatory culture," tracing the ways our own thinking has evolved through the years in response to a changing media environment and to the shifting stakes in policy debates surrounding digital media. When the concept first emerged, no one knew what shape networked communication might take or how it would impact fields such as education or politics. After twenty years, we are in a somewhat different position, able to look back on what has changed and what has not changed as our culture has absorbed a range of new media platforms and practices. Throughout this book-long dialogue, the authors try to reconcile conflicting bids about what all of this means and where it may be going next.

The authors of this book – Henry Jenkins, Mimi Ito*, and danah boyd – came of age at different moments in the rise of participatory culture and have diverse scholarly orientations and histories. Despite our varied backgrounds, our professional pathways are intertwined because of shared concerns, commitments, and interests concerning the social and cultural implications of emerging media. We are friends and colleagues who have supported, challenged, and collaborated with each other over the years.

More concretely, all three of us participated in the MacArthur Foundation's Digital Media and Learning initiative. Henry and his New Media Literacies team at MIT (Jenkins et al. 2007) developed a white paper that used the concept of participatory culture to describe the core social skills and cultural competencies that young people need to acquire in order to participate meaningfully in the new media landscape. Alongside Peter Lyman and Michael Carter, Mimi led a large-scale ethnographic study on youth, new media, and learning as part of this initiative; danah was brought in as one of the core graduate researchers on that study. Henry's New Media Literacy project and Mimi and danah's Digital Youth project were the first two major grants by MacArthur in what became the focus of the foundation's educational grant-making. Mimi and Henry have both served as participants in a MacArthur-funded research network focused on Youth and Participatory Politics, danah has worked with MacArthur on more policy-oriented research, and all three of us have worked together to help organize Digital Media and Learning conferences and mentorship programs.

The book reflects this history of working at the intersection of youth practices, participatory culture, and digital and networked technology. In addition to being the focus of our scholarly work, we believe this constellation of topics is timely and relevant as we navigate an

---

* Given the conversational nature of this book, Mizuko will be referred to throughout the text by the nickname "Mimi," the name by which she is most often referred to by friends and colleagues.

important shift in our media and communications environs. The focus on the relationship between participatory culture and digital and networked technology reflects the historical moment in which we write this book – as ideas around participation, crowdsourcing, peer production, and Web 2.0 are moving from geek culture to a more globalized mainstream. Young people remain a central focus of our research, in part because youth have been lead adopters of mobile, social, and gaming media. We see youth as uniquely positioned to effect social change, while also recognizing the conditions of oppression that they face in making their perspectives heard and appreciated. Our focus on the context of the US also deserves mention. While all of us have done international work, most notably Mimi in Japan, the center of gravity for our research has been in the US, and the book reflects this. Our discussions of US teens and the California tech scene no doubt reflect a degree of parochialism, but we hope these examples will have broader relevant readers outside of the US as well. We encourage scholars elsewhere to ask themselves similar questions about how these changes may be taking shape in their culturally specific contexts.

Each chapter in this book represents a shared topic of concern and begins with an introductory essay by one of the three authors, followed by a conversation between the three of us. Throughout, we weave together our personal experiences, perspectives, and research with a broader analysis of the issues at stake.

The first chapter, "Defining Participatory Culture," introduces the core concept framing this book. We then move, in "Youth Culture, Youth Practices," to a discussion of youth as a unique population that we have all studied in depth. From there, in "Gaps and Genres in Participation," we consider the diversity in forms of participation as it relates to issues of equity. These three chapters lay out the conceptual and topical terrain. There follow three chapters that delve more deeply into issues of concern and our investments as engaged public intellectuals. "Learning and Literacy" explores the implications of participatory culture for education and media literacy. "Commercial Culture" considers the complex dynamics between capitalism, popular culture, and today's networked media ecosystem. Finally, "Democracy, Civic Engagement, and Activism" considers the intersection between these topics and participatory and networked culture.

This book departs from scholarly convention in many ways, having come together through a dialogic and interactive process. The conversations reproduced here took place in Mimi's house in Los Angeles – the three of us sprawling on furniture, chomping on snacks, dealing with interruptions from children and neighbors, distracted by text messages and phone calls, but, slowly and surely, working through our shared agenda together. Along the way, we reached out to our own constituencies through Twitter and blogs, seeking questions they wanted us to address, and we've woven them into these dialogues. Over time, thanks to Google Docs, Microsoft Word, and Dropbox, we've edited, reorganized, debated, and filled in gaps in the original transcripts to give more structure and clarity to our originally rather informal exchanges. Evelyn McDonnell, Quinn Norton, and Matt Rafalow provided invaluable editorial input into this process, as did our editors at Polity Press, Andrea Drugan and Joe Devanny. While every book is a collective enterprise, this one has emerged from a particularly lively participatory process.

As you read the book, you will quickly realize that the conversations presented here reveal the ways in which the three of us, all deeply engaged in these issues, still struggle with many aspects of participatory culture. There are places where we disagree with each other and topics where we struggle analytically and intellectually. Unlike a typical scholarly manuscript, this book is about our willingness to reveal the limitations of our knowledge and our collective struggles to work out what we're privileged enough to witness. Research is a process, and all too often we tend to emphasize the final output. As scholars committed to participatory culture, we're also committed to opening up our practice and thinking. This book is our attempt to do just that. Enjoy!

Chapter 1

Defining Participatory Culture

Introduction by Henry Jenkins

More and more organizations, institutions, and businesses have embraced a rhetoric of participation, yet it is abundantly clear that not all forms of participation are equally meaningful or empowering. Many of the core debates of our time center around the terms of our participation: whether meaningful participation can occur under corporately controlled circumstances, when our ability to create and share content is divorced from our capacity to participate in the governance of the platforms through which that content circulates. Does participation become exploitation when it takes place on commercial platforms where others are making money off our participation and where we often do not even own the culture we are producing?

I first used the phrase "participatory culture" in *Textual Poachers* (Jenkins 1992), when I was contrasting participation with spectatorship; I was really only making descriptive claims about the cultural logic of fandom. *Poachers* described fans (in this case, mostly female fans of science fiction and other genre television programs) not simply as consumers of mass-produced content but also as a creative community that took its raw materials from commercial entertainment texts and appropriated and remixed them as the basis for their own creative culture. My book showcased the relationship between fans, texts, and producers but also the social relations that emerged within fandom as fans created a shared space where their own creative and critical interventions could be appropriately valued. This account of fan culture drew heavily on my own experiences of almost twenty years, at that point, of involvement in fan communities.

My ideas about culture come from Raymond Williams (1958), who defines culture as "ordinary," the "sum total of human experience," as everything that we as humans create or do together, from the most mundane aspects of our everyday lives to the most cherished expression of our artistic accomplishments or sacred beliefs. So, for me, a participatory culture describes what are sometimes very ordinary aspects of our lives in the digital age. A participatory culture is one which embraces the values of diversity and democracy through every aspect of our interactions with each other – one which assumes that we are capable of making decisions, collectively and individually, and that we should have the capacity to express ourselves through a broad range of different forms and practices.

My initial use of "participatory culture" to refer to fandom (Jenkins 1992) relied on a not fully conscious blurring between forms of cultural production and forms of social exchange; fans understood fandom to be an informal "community" defined around notions of equality, reciprocity, sociality, and diversity. The fans had a clear and (largely) shared understanding of what they were participating in and how their production and circulation of media content contributed to their shared well-being. And there was a clear tension between their culture and that of the commercial industries from which they took their raw materials. In this context, there are strong links between interpretation, production, curation, and circulation as potentially meaningful forms of participation.

The world I described in *Textual Poachers* was undergoing transition, as a community based on photocopiers, the postal service, and face-to-face encounters was giving way to electronically networked communications. At the same time, I was undergoing my own transition, starting work at the Massachusetts Institute of Technology (MIT) in 1989 during the first phases of the digital revolution. My work on fandom came out, for example, alongside Howard Rheingold's early writings about virtual communities (Rheingold 1993). At MIT, I had a ringside seat for debates about the role of new media in education, the promises of digital democracy, and the creative potentials of hypertext and interactive games. More and more people were using the concept of participatory culture to describe the new forms of cultural production and media-sharing that were taking shape in the early days of the internet. Much of what I was seeing in the emerging cyberculture reminded me of my own experiences in fandom. Critics of *Convergence Culture* (2006) have argued that I saw the new media landscape as fandom writ large, and I suspect this is a more or less fair criticism of where I was at when I wrote the book. I was not wrong to see fandom as one important element shaping contemporary participatory culture. Fans were often early adopters of new media platforms and practices and experimenters with modes of media-making. They were historically among the first to interact within geographically dispersed communities of interest. But they were simply one among many different kinds of communities that had been struggling throughout the twentieth century to gain greater access to the means of cultural production and circulation.

By the time I became involved in the MacArthur Digital Media and Learning initiative in 2005, my thinking about participatory culture operated on a much different scope and scale. I saw us entering an era when the public, at least in the developed world, would have access to much greater communicative capacity than ever before, where a growing number of institutions were embracing more participatory practices, and where the skills and knowledge to participate meaningfully were unevenly distributed. I examined a range of different sites of participatory culture in order to identify the ways they were supporting peer-to-peer mentorship and were encouraging and scaffolding participants as they refined their skills and developed greater confidence in their own voices. The white paper *Confronting the Challenges of a Participatory Culture* (Jenkins et al. 2007), written for MacArthur, was addressed to educators and adopted a definition of participatory culture that places a strong emphasis on its pedagogical potentials:

A participatory culture is a culture with relatively low barriers to artistic expression and civic engagement, strong support for creating and sharing one's creations, and some type of informal mentorship whereby what is known by the most experienced is passed along to novices. A participatory culture is also one in which members believe their contributions matter, and feel some degree of social connection with one another (at the least they care what other people think about what they have created).

Embracing Participatory Culture

Mimi: I was very influenced by Henry's work on fandom and his early writing on gaming when I was doing my dissertation work on children's software. It empowered me to pursue work on the participatory dimensions of media culture at a time when digital and online media were still emergent and not the focus of much scholarly attention. Back then, I wouldn't have positioned Henry as a researcher in my field of learning sciences, but I already saw the relevance. I was thrilled when he started doing more and more work that was explicitly educational, looking to participatory culture for a set of positive values for learning and literacy. It was probably overdetermined by our backgrounds and interests, but Henry, Howard Rheingold, and I found ourselves seeing similar kinds of opportunities for participation and learning emerging from new digital and networked media. Where Henry focused on fans, I've tended to focus on geeks, but it feels part of a similar family and a shared tendency to celebrate certain kinds of activated media engagements.

Unlike Henry, however, I came at these issues through the learning sciences, not media studies. As a graduate student at Stanford, I worked out of the Institute for Research on Learning (IRL), where Lave and Wenger (1991) had written their *Situated Learning* book together. IRL was a research institute that focused on social and cultural studies of learning. Unlike traditional views of learning, which

4

focus on pouring content into the heads of kids in a standardized and individualized way, this approach sees learning as an act of participation in communities of shared culture and practice. These theories of learning and participation grew out of anthropological work in settings where learning is embedded in the everyday life of communities rather than sequestered into educational institutions, and it's not accidental that we've all found ourselves working at a similar intersection. And we've benefited from the MacArthur Foundation's Digital Media and Learning initiative giving us a context and resources for working together.

danah: I was first exposed to the notion of "participatory culture" when I took classes from Henry in graduate school at MIT. Then I moved to San Francisco in January 2003 and embedded myself within a network of entrepreneurs and geeks who would go on to form the start-ups that became the backbone of what is now described as "Web 2.0." The emic language used in these crowds was that of "user-generated content." As I listened to what they were envisioning and what they were trying to create, I realized that the startup scene was imagining many of the same things that Henry had turned me on to. Initially, this crowd had many of the same sensibilities as the fan communities that Henry encountered – subcultural resistance mixed with the particular narratives of liberty that Biella Coleman (2013) picks up on in *Coding Freedom*, where there was a political desire to have software be free as in freedom, not free as in beer. But a lot of this is now forgotten. Where we're sitting now – with Facebook having become a public company, marketers trying to make memes go viral, and social media being a worldwide phenomenon – it's hard to remember what San Francisco was like even a few years ago.

Mimi: Ideas about participatory culture and communities of practice have spread and morphed radically in the years since I was in graduate school. What was once a set of theories at the margins of academia is now part of a common vocabulary in some sectors of the industry and in much of media studies and the learning sciences. As a more wide-ranging set of players started to engage with these ideas, it has forced a set of conversations about what counts as participatory culture or a community of practice. For example, many of the early studies of situated learning and communities of practice centered on relatively defined, face-to-face professional communities, such as tailors (Lave 2011), butchers (Lave and Wenger 1991), and copier technicians (Orr 1996). What does it mean to apply these ideas about learning and participation to classrooms, online communities, and large corporate work teams? Now an acronym, "CoPs," communities of practice have become a familiar buzzword among managers seeking to build cohesion and sharing in work teams. These shifts have been a source of consternation to some of the pioneers in situated learning theory who feel the ideas have been watered down or misappropriated. It's heartening to see these frameworks resonate more broadly, but they've also fallen victim to their own success. Can we hold onto the core values that animated the early years of situated learning theory and participatory culture while also appreciating how they have spread and evolved?

Henry: I came to Lave and Wenger and the other CoP thinkers somewhat later. My own initial thinking about education and participation was influenced early on by one of my MIT colleagues, Seymour Papert. Papert (1975) had written about his visit to a samba school in Rio. The samba schools were informal gathering places where people living in a community developed their performances for next year's carnival. Papert stressed the informal circumstances through which dancers of very different levels of experience collaborated to construct collective performances. He asked whether educators might incorporate some of those same processes into the design and practice of schooling. Papert celebrated these moments of collective creativity, in part because his whole constructivist education paradigm emphasizes active participation and de-emphasizes formalized teaching.

When I went to Rio a few years ago, I visited one of the samba schools and I came away with a clearer sense of what Papert was talking about. At any given moment, there are many different modes of engagement: some are watching and observing, waiting to participate, while others are on the floor dancing and others are much more peripheral, watching from the balcony and texting their friends. There are announcers on a sound system actively soliciting participation, coaxing shy community members onto the dance floor. At one point, a group of people in what looked like police or military uniforms step-marched through the space, grabbing people they suspected of not contributing to the collective effort. Eager to avoid being "arrested," I asked my host what to do, and he suggested putting on a festive T-shirt we had been given at the door. He figured that, even if I couldn't dance, I could at least be decorative. This was a great reminder both of the many different ways participants might contribute and of the need sometimes to invite, encourage, and, in this case, even coerce participation rather than take it for granted.

Mimi: Most forms of learning are much more integrated with the dynamic life of communities than our current formal education system. The samba school is a nice example of that. Even in our post-industrial society, most learning is still seamless with everyday life and sociability, whether it is picking up our first language, learning to cook, or figuring out how to build a house in Minecraft. The challenge is when these different modes of learning collide. Kids fail in their studies or get left out from collective practices because they don't have the necessary cultural knowledge or experience. Most educational settings aren't as successful as the samba school at meeting learners where they are and inviting different contributions. Whether it is in a classroom or a professional community of practice, we often see exclusion and marginality operating in less friendly ways when different ways of doing things butt up against one another. Often those dynamics that promote the cohesion of the "in" group are also barriers to entry for learners and newcomers.

Henry: As the samba school example reminds us, many core principles of participatory learning might have been understood by previous generations of folk artists. My grandmother was a remix artist: she was a quilter. She would take bits of remaindered cloth from the local textile mills and use them to create something new. She was able to express herself meaningfully through the appropriation and recombination of borrowed materials. She would have learned these skills informally, observing the community of quilting women as they worked, gradually trying her own hands at the craft and learning through doing. Skills, knowledge, and traditions were passed from generation to generation.

These forms of creative expression were woven into the practices of everyday life. Yet, she was living in a society that was segregated by class and race and, in this case, also by gender. For her, quilting would have been her entry into a white, working-class, female culture, a source of solidarity with others in her community, but hardly open to all. And it is hard to visit the samba schools and not see them in relation to the economic and educational poverty and often racial segregation that surrounds them. So, in some ways, our goal of more diverse and inclusive communities of practice sets higher standards than anyone had achieved in the past.

That said, we might see the samba schools as an example of the ways aspects of traditional folk cultures persist in the eras of mass media and digital culture. As I suggested in *Convergence Culture* (Jenkins 2006), folk culture was disrupted by the rise of mass spectator culture across the twentieth century, but some aspects are returning in an age of digital culture. I am often asked whether all cultures are participatory, and the answer is that different configurations of culture invite or enable different degrees of participation. With digital culture, more people are making media and sharing what they made with each other. Grassroots and amateur forms of expression gained much greater visibility. Just as my grandmother took bits of cloth from the textile mills and remixed them, my friends and students take bits of media and stitch them together to create something new.

Right now, folk culture, mass culture, and digital culture co-exist. If we go back to the samba school, carnival takes on many of the traits of mass culture when it is broadcast on national television, thus shifting the focus from the yearlong process of getting ready to the specific event that is consumed as a product. You suddenly have many more consumers and potentially fewer participants, and the event gets inserted into a state or commercial context.

Now, consider what happens when we insert some of the mechanisms of the samba schools into a digital context. We are seeing street dancers, either individuals or in groups, across Brazil, create short YouTube videos demonstrating their moves to each other across a much more dispersed geography. Dance moves travel from one community to another with high speed and fluidity – indeed, the videos can travel to places where the dancers themselves could not safely go. The performers may well be dancing to mass-produced songs, and they may well be distributing their work through commercially owned platforms. But the ways they are producing these videos do not radically differ from earlier folk practices, except in the scope and scale of their circulation.

danah: As more corporations capitalize on people's practices, we've seen a significant shift in power. Although Henry's original work was intended to recognize and celebrate the practices of fans in response to media companies, the new media companies are now capitalizing directly on people's participation. This, in turn, angers many cultural critics, who reject the term "participatory culture" as outright capitalistic, failing to recognize the very cultural logic underpinning people's activities in the first place. As time has passed, my experiences with – and understanding of – participatory culture have become wrapped up in the tensions brought about by commercialization, even as I watch youth engage for personal, educational, political, and social reasons.

I've come to think that the making of culture is inherently participatory, but I appreciate Henry's efforts to point out that this continues to be true in a media-saturated world where many people think that we are passive consumers of culture. (This was certainly true for TV and, to a lesser degree, the early internet.) Part of my struggle with the term itself is that Henry and Mimi both did a phenomenal job of illustrating this through many rarified practices (e.g., fan fiction, machinima) in ways that resulted in the concept of participatory culture being tied to those practices. I see mainstream practices – such as taking selfies for Instagram (or even more challenging practices like collectively producing a how-to-be-anorexic guide) – as deeply engaged cultural production too, but these are not the kinds of things that normally get labeled as "participatory culture," even if you would see them as such. This is one of the challenges of intending one thing when constructing a concept and then having it repurposed by others in unexpected ways. As a result, for better or worse, my general tendency is to avoid the phrase except when speaking specifically about your work on specific participatory culture activities.

Henry: I have no problem in thinking of taking selfies (or participating in online forums, regardless of the topics) as "ordinary" forms of participatory culture. I don't think the term refers simply to sub-cultures structured around specific forms of participation; it would certainly include more routine practices like taking selfies, though to be participatory these activities have to involve meaningful connections to some larger community (even if only the cohort of classmates at the local school). Part of the nature of networked culture is that even forms of expression that might have had a very limited audience in the past now travel through networks and thus have bigger social consequences.

I also do not assume that participatory culture always has positive effects, so pro-ana sites are a great example of a community that probably meets all of my criteria for participatory culture but does not necessarily make the world a better place.

Participatory Media Platforms?

Mimi: As we see the term "participatory culture" migrate to other uses, such as logging clicks on a social network site, it's important to be clearer about its meaning. Henry, you say the concept of participation involves a cluster of characteristics that we took for granted. If we look at your pre-digital work on fan culture, or Lave and Wenger's work on participation, it is about being part of shared social practices, not just engaging with an online platform or piece of content. Looked at this way, participation doesn't just mean being active, it is also about being part of a shared practice and culture. Many technology-centric uses of the term implicitly define participation through the use of a platform, or a site, rather than a shared practice or culture. This is a critical distinction in what we mean by participatory culture versus how the term can often get used in the technology world. Henry's early work on fandom is a good example of strongly shared practice and culture that relied on conventions, snail mail, and non-digital media. I wouldn't say that today's more digital fandoms are more participatory, but the new technology has made it easier to access longstanding fan practices of the sort the Henry looked at in the 1980s.

Henry: There's been a tendency in some high-tech circles to act as if participatory culture originated with YouTube or social networking with Facebook. Instead, we need to place these practices in a larger historical context. My grandmother's quilting was grounded in her lived realities, in the ways she worked, worshiped, and socialized with people in her immediate geographic vicinity. She and the other women were linked by a complex set of ties, including shared experience of poverty, which made it essential for them to construct their lives together. Such deep ties may or may not be experienced by those who are producing and sharing media content in today's online communities. Certainly, many teens associate online with people they encounter face to face in their own neighborhoods; others form strong emotional bonds with people they regularly encounter online. But there is an option simply to walk away from many of the communities we encounter online, which make them different from the world my grandmother grew up in as a poor dirt farmer in the American South, or from the favela residents in Rio's samba schools.

Though the term is often ascribed to me, I avoid the phrase "participatory media." I do not think technologies are participatory; cultures are. Technologies may be interactive in their design; they may facilitate many-to-many communications; they may be accessible and adaptable to multiple kinds of users; and they may encode certain values through their terms of use and through their interfaces. But, ultimately, those technologies get embraced and deployed by people who are operating in cultural contexts that may be more or less participatory. I do not think of platforms like Facebook or YouTube as participatory cultures. Rather, they are tools participatory communities sometimes use as means of maintaining social contact or sharing their cultural productions with each other.

We might understand what I mean by participation in contrast to the term "interactivity," with which it is often confused. Interactivity refers to the properties of technologies that are designed to enable users to make meaningful choices (as in a game) or choices that may personalize the experience (as in an app). Participation, on the other hand, refers to properties of the culture, where groups collectively and individually make decisions that have an impact on their shared experiences. We participate *in* something; we interact *with* something. There is clearly some overlap between the two, so, when someone clicks a button on a social media site, the interface is designed to enable their interactivity, whereas what they post might contribute to a larger process of deliberation and participation within the community.

Mimi: Prior to working on anime fandom, my work centered on games, online groups, and learning. I didn't use the term "participatory culture" to describe those practices. I used the term "interactive media" to designate the difference between games and multimedia that I was studying at the time and media forms such as books and television. This is similar to how Henry has described interactivity, in that it is a property of media technology, not practice. I was also studying online, networked groups and used the term "network communities" to designate the groups we were studying such as forums and online gamers. My conceptual vocabulary has tended to lean towards building distinctions between networked social forms and non-networked forms to answer the question of what is "new" about today's media. By contrast, the term "participatory culture" raises the question of what constitutes different levels or forms of engagement. It's important not to conflate the two by assuming that new interactive and networked media are always more participatory or engaging. The term "participatory culture" is valuable in helping us distinguish between different forms of engagement with similar media. It's not whether it is books or television or games that matters for participatory culture, but how people are engaging with those media. I would also agree that taking selfies or being part of a pro-ana forum are examples of participatory culture. While there is a clear history of being associated with more nerdy content communities, I don't see any reason why the term needs to be restricted to them.

Participation is inherent in all forms of social practice. I would not want our use of "participatory culture" to imply that there are forms of culture that don't involve participation. I saw a similar dynamic with the term "situated learning," which was intended to signify how all learning is situated in culture and social practice. Often people would talk about how classroom learning was "not situated learning" when, in my view, even the most traditional classroom learning is situated, just in a different set of contexts than what you see in kids' peer culture or in the home.

Participation and Resistance

Henry: Going back to danah's experience in early 2000s San Francisco, any understanding of participatory culture today has to factor in the wave of commercialization that has impacted contemporary digital culture. Because some of the ideals of participatory cultures got so encoded into the language of the digital industries, it is increasingly difficult to imagine what a more "authentic" form of participation might look like. At the start, writers in the cultural studies tradition (see, for example, Cherny and Weise 1996) were drawn towards the internet for models of cultural resistance – ways that alternative online communities might challenge the control of powerful institutions or might pose critiques of the ideologies being circulated within commercial culture. My work, from the start, sought to describe a complex relationship between fans and the culture around them. Fandom is born out of fascination and some frustration. If you weren't fascinated, you wouldn't continue to engage as a fan. If you weren't frustrated, you often wouldn't continue to rewrite and reinvent.

In *Spreadable Media* (Jenkins, Ford, and Green 2013), we make the argument that, today, an emphasis on participation has displaced this focus on resistance. There can be no easy separation between fans and producers; more and more, media producers embrace our participation as a means of increasing engagement in a highly competitive media system. Yet they also seek to shape and direct our participation into forms that they see as serving their own interests. I think the language shift from resistance to participation comes with some implications. Resistance to what? Participation in what? Participation implies some notion of affiliation, collective identity, membership, but, beyond that, we have much to figure out if we are going to continue to apply this framework to contemporary digital culture.

danah: We're all personally and politically drawn to communities that are resistant, but I want to take Henry's notion of "Resistant to what?" seriously. Does participatory culture have to be resistant to the status quo? And do communities have to form out of participatory culture or can people be a part of participatory culture without developing the deep connections that both of you highlight in your work?

Henry: My understanding of the term "resistance" comes from the Birmingham School of Cultural Studies (Hall and Jefferson 1993). It goes back to their original work on subcultures and appropriation. They were writing about the punk movement and the manner in which it appropriated and remixed symbols belonging to the dominant culture, often in ways that signaled their opposition to core institutions and values of their parents' generation. So, Dick Hebdidge (1979) and Stuart Hall (1981) use the example of the swastika, which, for the punks, was chosen not because they were Nazis (many of them were strongly anti-fascist) but because they knew that their parents had survived the Blitz and that this symbol was thus sure to set their mums' and dads' teeth on edge. Hall argues that, if this highly charged symbol can be up for grabs, then any and all signs can be appropriated and reworked for expressive purposes.

Over time, the term "resistance" came to refer to symbolic gestures that questioned or challenged the values of the status quo. So, we might talk about feminist or queer appropriations of materials from mass media that encouraged the questioning of patriarchy or allowed for the expression of alternative sexual politics. These forms of resistance might be oppositional in the ways that media is produced and distributed, participating in an alternative economy which rejected the profit motive or refused to accept constraints on its use of intellectual property. These groups could be oppositional in the sense that they encouraged alternative social structures based on equality, diversity, and reciprocity or a refusal to make money off other community members. They could be oppositional in terms of the symbols used, the meanings their work evoked, or the ways their media practices pushed against censorship norms and taboos of the culture. Historically, subcultures defined their identities in opposition to their parent cultures. This focus on opposition differs from the ways I write about the samba schools, where we are seeing forms of folk production that are normative in Brazilian culture, or the ways we might now talk about niche culture, which may be distinctive to a particular group but positively valued within the creative economy.

I am not sure that digital cultures, of the kinds we are discussing as participatory culture, are necessarily oppositional or resistant in the same way that the British Cultural Studies writers discussed the teddy boys or the punks (Hebdidge 1979; McRobbie 1991). For one thing, these earlier writers had a much clearer sense of a dominant or mainstream culture against which to define these subcultures, whereas a growing body of research (Bennett and Kahn-Harris 2004; Muggleton and Weinzierl 2004) suggests the fragmentation of contemporary culture and the emergence of niche communities. There may no longer be a unified mainstream culture against which subcultures can define themselves. So, when we talk about niches, we may be describing divisions in a commercial market as much as or more than divisions in the culture.

That said, these communities may represent alternatives which, for young people, frequently get defined in relation to school, family life, their work lives, etc. Often, they are alternative in that they represent different structures of knowledge, status and reputation, or norms and values. Someone who has very little power at home might emerge as a guild leader in an online game world. Someone who is a poor student at school may be seen as an expert in their online community. Someone with limited freedom at work may be respected as a fan fiction writer. These are not resistant in that they overturn existing structures. But they may be alternative in that they provide participants with the social capital or self-esteem needed to survive other constraints they confront.

danah: My usage of the term "resistance" is rooted in this exact history, including more modern work that builds off this trajectory such as analyses of goth subcultures (Hodkinson 2002) and queer counterpublics (Warner 2002). But I also think of it in terms of agency and power in relation to technological artifacts and their creators. I don't see technologies as predicting behavior, but I do see technology creators as trying to corral users into a narrow range of acceptable activities. And I love watching youth recognize this and push back, reorient, repurpose, or otherwise resist the system designers' expectations.

For example, I enjoyed watching teenagers when they started to realize that Facebook's news feed algorithm resulted in their not seeing everything their friends posted. They worked out – accurately or not – that posting brand names or links to Buzzfeed articles resulted in their postings appearing to be more likely to show up on their friends' feeds. So you'd see posts like "Yo wazzup? Nike. I'm bored." They were "tricking" the algorithm to get what they wanted out of the system. I see this as an act of resistance or an effort to reclaim power and control within a socio-technical context in which that is often taken away.

Mimi: I also see "resistance" as a relational term that is predicated on there being a perceived or structural kind of dominance. In the case of subcultures that are defined in opposition to mainstream culture, yes, I would call that resistant. Like Henry, I study a lot of cultural forms that are niche but not "resistant," because they don't have that stance of opposition. Environmentalism, geek culture, fan culture, and other "alternative" cultural movements and identities are often defined as explicitly distinct from a mainstream culture but are also not explicitly resistant to that culture. In otaku culture, for example, I would not call kids who make fan manga about a mainstream franchise like Naruto "resistant," but I would say some of the young women who depict alternative narratives that explicitly challenge gender norms are resistant. Similarly I would say a lot of gaming culture is niche and participatory but not resistant. When young people are pushing back against parental or school authority, I would call that resistant because it is a response to institutionalized power and inequity. And technology operates in a similar way because it can occupy a position of structural dominance.

Henry: The digital did not make fandom more participatory, but the digital did dramatically expand who got to participate in fandom. Fandom has a culture of participation that spans 150 years. So we could go back to the toy printing press movement of the mid-nineteenth century, where kids were hand-setting type to create newsletters and other kinds of publications – what we might today call zines. These spread across an informal and national network of people who shared common passions but who might never have met face to face. Some of those same people also became part of the amateur radio movement in the early twentieth century. Out of amateur radio emerged the beginnings of science fiction fandom, which borrowed terminology, practices, and infrastructure from the National Amateur Press Association. Skip forward a few years and some of these people contributed to the underground newspapers, the people's radio, and the underground comics of the 1960s counterculture. Many helped to define the ideals of participatory democracy which were very much part of the student movements of that era. And then, in the 1980s, we might point to the emergence of the camcorder and local access television as a site of grassroots cultural production and a platform for alternative politics. DIY culture, more broadly, was associated with the counterculture going back to the beatniks of the 1950s. These same impulses helped to define the early internet culture – the culture of amateurs, hackers, and home brew.

I am discussing this in terms of fans, because I know of generations within the same family that map these movements across different sites of popular media production, and I know that some of the terminology associated with the Amateur Press Association (LOL, for example) still functions as part of the language of contemporary digital culture. In practice, though, many groups followed similar paths, struggling to find channels of communication through which they could express their political and cultural perspectives.

So, when we look at YouTube today, we see various forms of media production which have a much older history within diverse cultural and subcultural communities. YouTube offers them certain affordances for sharing their media with each other, but the participatory practices originated elsewhere. YouTube might be seen as simply one point in the much longer trajectory towards a more participatory culture.

For some, YouTube functions as an informal and personal archive, with videos being seen by relatively few other people. For others, YouTube, as Sarah Banet-Wiser (2012) has suggested, represents a vehicle for personal branding, where the goal is to get noticed by as many people as possible. For yet others, though, YouTube is a site of exchange within a particular subcultural community using video-making to contribute to the group's ongoing conversation among the group's members. Beyond this, YouTube and the other Web 2.0 platforms are what Yochai Benkler (2007) might describe as hybrid media ecologies, where media producers with many different goals – amateur, commercial, semiprofessional, activist, educational, religious, governmental – operate side by side. Media practices move fluidly from one community to another within this shared space. Media producers learn from each other and build on each other's work.

Mimi: YouTube is part of a whole ecology of openly networked platforms supporting the spread of amateur and noncommercial media production and sharing communities. What's interesting about the communities being built through openly networked platforms is that anyone can potentially contribute and have a voice, but what you actually see is people creating new kinds of boundaries and status hierarchies. People find ways of signaling status and difference even within a very flat and peer-to-peer structure. In fact, these two dimensions are interrelated. Because these platforms have reduced the barriers to initial entry and participation, communities that care about shared norms and quality of work need to develop ways of signaling expectations and status. As a result, one irony is that exclusionary forms of social and cultural capital, your identity and who you know, become much more important than traditional institutional status. People find ways of defining who belongs by culture, style, and social networks, and it can be harder to break into the "elite" of a group than into a purely market-based or more transparent institutional hierarchy or status system. This is one of the new dangers with how participatory communities define who is in or out.

I've been looking at otaku culture, or fandoms centered around Japanese popular media, as another instance of these cases (Ito, Okabe, and Tsuji 2012). Interesting things happen when a longstanding fandom moves into the digital era. What you've seen is a huge expansion of overseas fans of anime into an international subculture – what Clay Shirky (2006) has described as a mega-niche. In many ways this has broadened the base and enriched the fandom. For US fans of anime, for example, it used to be really hard to get access to the media content, and it took a certain intensity and commitment to be part of the fandom. But now anime is on cable, and anyone can watch it streaming on the internet, and suddenly what used to be insider knowledge and cult media have become much more accessible. This has also meant that old-timers and highly expert fans have developed new ways of signaling subcultural capital, to differentiate themselves from the newer, younger, and less sophisticated fans (Ito 2012a). We've seen similar dynamics at play with Wikipedians maintaining quality standards (Swartz 2006) or how reputation works among players who modify games (modders), and the open source programming scene (e.g., Kow and Nardi 2010; Lakhani and Wolf 2005; Weber 2005). It's a good lesson as to how, even with very open, participatory cultures with low barriers to entry, people find ways of maintaining status and distinction.

danah: Your examples highlight the subcultural roots of this practice, where a small group of people – e.g., fans – are able to create ways of engaging deeply. I think it's important to celebrate such spaces, but does it make sense for this to go mainstream? What is gained and what is lost when these practices "jump the shark" or become commonplace? Will the aspects of participatory culture that you relish actually translate well into the mainstream? Or will things get distorted in uncomfortable ways? Can technologies drive participatory culture or does it require a particular mindset? For example, I would argue that sites like Facebook and YouTube can be used by people engaged in participatory culture but, by and large, engagement on these sites – including "user-generated content" – is nothing more than mediated sociality.

Mimi: The subcultural origins of the term are incredibly important for signaling the relationship between, say, fans and industry. I don't feel that the participatory culture has to be subcultural to be valuable, though, particularly when we consider learning. When you think about what is important for learning and development, it's the act of creation and contribution to a shared purpose that is most important, not whether the culture is mainstream or subcultural.

It's worth thinking too of how so-called mainstream cultures also have participatory elements. For example, Henry, you look at fandoms that have grown around very broad-based commercial media content such as *American Idol*. I tend to get some raised eyebrows when I talk about a case that one of our team members is currently looking at, centered on the fans of the hugely popular boy band One Direction (Korobkova 2013). While the more participatory elements of such fandoms may push back on the more top-down and commercially defined notions of audience participation, I am not sure I would describe these fandoms as oppositional or even "alternative," though they exhibit elements of participatory culture.

Henry: I would make two points. First, you are right that mainstream media are increasingly adopting participatory practices in hopes of intensifying audience engagement with their properties. As a consequence, cultural activities that once seemed "alternative" are becoming part of the dominant logic through which media industries operate. So, "voting" for *American Idol* is a form of participation that cannot be described as resistant or alternative but is also highly regulated and controlled from above.

Second, within such dominant or mainstream practices, there are nevertheless forms of participation that do constitute space for alternative interests. In the case of *American Idol*, one geeky bunch of people are trying to figure out whether the voting is rigged. There is another even more oppositional group – Vote for the Worst – that seeks to throw their collective weight behind "bad singers" in order to force the producers to keep them on the air longer and thus undermine Fox's commercial interests. Neither of these groups would be described as dominant or mainstream, even if they direct their energies towards a property that was among the highest-rated television series for most of the decade. They are also not in a strong sense oppositional; we might describe them perhaps as disruptive or critical but, nevertheless, negotiating a space for their interests within the commercial culture. No matter how participatory culture is pulled towards dominant practices, it cannot close off space for other, less mainstream interests if it is going to remain truly participatory.

Towards a More Participatory Culture

danah: I definitely see the power of participatory culture for more alternative communities, but the rhetoric surrounding social media often highlights that technology is an equal opportunity platform; "everyone" supposedly has the ability to have their voice heard. I think that this is seriously deceptive. I would argue that true participation requires many qualities: agency, the ability to understand a social situation well enough to engage constructively, the skills to contribute effectively, connections with others to help build an audience, emotional resilience to handle negative feedback, and enough social status to speak without consequences. The barrier to participation is not the technology but the kinds of privilege that are often ignored in meritocratic discourse. I do think that technology has opened up new doors to some people – and especially those who are marginalized but self-empowered (a.k.a. the alternative/resistant folks you're describing) – but it's important to recognize the ways in which it also reinforces other forms of inequalities that make it harder for some people to engage.

Henry: This is in part why I see participation more and more in relational rather than absolute terms – a matter of degree rather than of difference. So, yes, all culture is in some sense participatory, but the more hierarchical a culture is, the less participatory it becomes. I am today more likely to talk about a shift towards "a more participatory culture." It would be easy to assume that I'm saying that we already live in a fully participatory culture. We might instead see participatory culture as a set of ideals, a kind of social structure we are collectively striving to achieve, a collection of aspirations about what a better cultural configuration might look like. There are both social and technological obstacles to full participation at the current moment.

Talking about a movement towards a more participatory culture allows us to acknowledge the ongoing struggle of many different groups to gain greater access to the means of cultural production and circulation. It allows us to take stock of the ground we've made but also to acknowledge that many people are not able to participate meaningfully. And we are still struggling over the terms of our participation. There is always a risk that the more participatory dimensions of our culture may not survive.

Even if these new media platforms offer us affordances that can be used in support of a more participatory culture, they also often impose constraints on how they can be used or erect barriers to equal and meaningful participation. This new culture is porous, meaning that media move from one community to another, often bringing into contact people who have no history of interacting with each other – what danah often discusses as context collapse. As a result, there are often serious conflicts that further marginalize some people while increasing the visibility enjoyed by more dominant groups. We do not yet have well-defined norms, or shared values, that allow us to deal with some of these situations – and perhaps we never will. For me, a commitment to participatory culture demands a commitment to overcome these various participation gaps.

What's at Stake?

danah: Part of what I love about participatory culture is that it shifts the locus of control and destabilizes systems of power, but I wouldn't go as far as calling it inherently democratizing. New sources of power, status, and control emerge and introduce new forms of inequality. This is a serious source of concern for those who have seen their positions of power undermined, particularly when they see problematic dynamics bubble up. And, while the activist punk in me wants to stick out my tongue and offer my middle finger, I'm also aware that anarchy doesn't always result in positive outcomes. I can't help but reflect on cases where participatory culture has resulted in negative outcomes for individuals, communities, and public life – where misinformation can go unchecked and be widely disseminated to mislead, manipulate, or induce fear, where hate speech proliferates and has serious consequences. This is not to say that these issues are unique to participatory culture. Propaganda and the Ku Klux Klan certainly pre-date participatory culture. Still, I'd argue that participatory culture enables – if not empowers – disturbing practices alongside positive ones. I believe in participatory culture because of its potential, and I don't want to see negative outcomes or fears being used to justify centralized control or censorship – but nor do I want the hopeful vision to gloss over or otherwise ignore the darker side of things. You have to grapple with the ugliness to make sure that naysayers don't stifle the potential.

Mimi: Participation is part of a broader value set associated with network culture, which includes other values like transparency and openness. The three of us have somewhat different voices in these debates, even while we're all looking towards the similar positive future. I appreciate voices saying, "Look, here are the limits of transparency, here are the negative outcomes of participation." I don't see those voices as at all hostile to the world that I want to see, but also want to keep the positive value set in view as an ideal. We can celebrate the human agency, inclusiveness, and accessibility that come with participatory values, even as we need to recognize costs and unanticipated consequences.

danah: Recognizing that I share your values and goals, help me understand something. From your perspective, what's the cost of *not* promoting participatory culture?

Mimi: We've been experiencing the cost of non-participatory systems, which center on inequitable access to the means of cultural production and distribution, which in turn are tied in important ways to social and political empowerment. When creating knowledge and culture is associated with elites, it tracks in troubling ways to historical forms of stratification based on things like socio-economic status and race. It means that certain populations have fewer avenues to contribute meaningfully to public life and culture and find a fulfilling place for themselves in society. I see this most concretely in learning and literacy, where privileged young people are given more opportunities to take on influential forms of cultural production and public participation tied to institutionalized power and wealth. This can be through success in schooling as well as through the whole host of enrichment activities in athletics, arts, and other areas of interest. All young people have agency and voice, but not everyone has the opportunity to connect this agency and voice to a broader public stage and to sites of power. This is where I think participatory and network culture has the potential to address some of this inequity.

Henry: For me, the value of a participatory culture is bound up with two core concepts. Both can be empty signifiers, overused to the point of banality, but they may also be the most significant things we could fight for. One is democracy; the other is diversity. If we enable all citizens to have a voice in their society, then there's a fundamental shift in governance. Ensuring that all those voices are heard is the best mechanism for dealing with the multiplicity and diversity of a global society. Those are the two values that drive me to fight for participation. How do we ensure that citizens have greater voice in the decision-making that impacts their life, and how do we ensure that people of diverse perspectives are heard by each other and benefit from each other's insights?

Right now, we are at a moment of transition. For many of us, we are experiencing a significant expansion of our communicative capacities within a networked culture, yet very little in our past has taught us how to use those expanded capacities responsibly or constructively. If that transition takes place, it's bound to be enormously disruptive. It's confusing, there are ethical dilemmas, none of us know how to use that power. I always quote what Uncle Ben tells his nephew Peter Parker in the *Spider-Man* comics: "With great power comes great responsibility."

Ideally, we are developing personal and collective ethics. We're thinking through the implication of our communicative acts. We are learning to take ownership over misinformation or malicious speech. We are starting to call each other out for the ways in which one group silences another. We can't say participation is good in and of itself. As we make these lurches towards using that power responsibly, we as a society make mistakes. There are people abusing this emerging freedom and groups that have trouble communicating to each other. It's a messy business. The only way forward is to ask the hard questions, to confront the bad along with the good, to challenges the inequalities and the abuses.

There has been a regrettable tendency for some critics of participatory culture (Janissary Collective 2012) to read these self-policing functions of communities largely in negative terms ("public shaming," "coercive participation," "surveillance culture", "governmentality") – as somehow oppositional to the "freedom" of their individual members. While such shared norms can manifest themselves as, for example, heteronormativity or privilege, and we thus need to critically question norms as they start to emerge, I still feel that shared ethical norms may be the most effective way of ensuring both a culture that respects the contributions of diverse participants and that the group can work towards mutual goals. Given the degree to which progressive politics has always rested on some notion of the collective interest, it seems dangerous to define individualism as the only viable source of freedom. It can also seem circular, since the critique of neoliberalism often rests on the belief that it reduces society to a collection of self-interested individuals.

danah: I wholeheartedly agree with your goals of diversity and democracy, but I think that you allude to another tension at play here. On the one hand, you have the liberal commitment to the public good and, on the other, a form of hyper-individualism that is often antithetical to collective narratives. Consider Alice Marwick's (2013) work investigating the rhetoric and norms of tech industry players at the onset of "Web 2.0." She argues that the values embedded in many of the technologies of participatory culture stem from meritocratic, libertarian, neoliberal beliefs. In other words, these tools are designed to empower – and value – individuals at the expense of the public good. This is instantiated in many technologies. For example, YouTube's mantra is "Broadcast Yourself." The emphasis is on valuing the individual and their right to self-expression, regardless of how that act affects others or of the costs for the public. The focus is on individual participation through performing, not through listening.

Henry: Many media platforms that describe themselves as participatory do not encourage the development of any collective understanding of cultural production. Sites like YouTube can be meeting grounds where multiple subcultures intersect, each bringing pre-existing media-making practices with them (Burgess and Green 2009), each learning from the other, but YouTube itself generates no shared identities or values, as is witnessed by the ruthless comments around YouTube posts. For many, there is no investment in building long-term relationships between participants. There's some argument to be made that video-blogging has started to emerge as a participatory community with strong social ties and collective interests (Lange 2014), but it is not clear that this community is bound to, or originates from, YouTube as a platform. Its practices have been strongly informed by grassroots, alternative media-production traditions of all kinds. And, through gatherings such as VidCon, we are seeing some subset of YouTubers start to work together towards larger civic, political, economic, and cultural goals. So, YouTube can be seen as a moving target in some senses, yet for many it is a place they go to consume videos (as if it were a broadcast channel), and they do not see themselves as having any real stakes in its community-like functions.

danah: I too believe that working out a shared vision of society by developing shared norms is tremendously valuable. And I believe that this *can* be done through technology. But I also believe that many of the systems that are widely used make it very difficult to see beyond a narrowly defined world. I've been fascinated by how the Trending Topics on Twitter often expose people to conversations and worlds outside of their network. But this can also backfire. Consider, for example, what happened in 2009 when all of the Trending Topics were icons of the black community during the Black Entertainment Television Awards. It was stunning how many white Twitter users responded to the appearance of black celebrities with racist commentary. These white users weren't used to seeing black users on Twitter. Rather than working to find common ground, they responded with hateful messages, preferring to live in their own white bubbles. If everyone today gets to build their own gated community because they can consume only the content of people like them and create their own communities of people who share their values, then what? How do we educate people about cultural differences? How do we get people to engage with communities that are different than theirs? Even education seems to be moving in the direction of individualism.

Networked Individualism?

danah: I want to believe that networks result in healthier communities, but I also think that they promote a form of egocentrism. Consider Barry Wellman's (1999) notion of "networked individualism." He uses that term in opposition to such traditional social structures as hierarchical organizations, families, neighborhoods, and peer groups. Unlike earlier technologies meant to organize people around groups, many social media tools allow people to cultivate networks. While there is overlap, my network on Twitter is different than yours, allowing us to define our own sense of community. This is super convenient, but it is also seriously narcissistic. What constitutes the public when we're each living in our personalized world? How do we engender public-good outcomes when our tools steer us towards individualism?

Henry: I grant you that the industry's discourse often stresses individualism. Neoliberalism is very much bound up with the notion of every person for themselves. But if we go back to fan culture, it's about collective ownership of stories, about sharing economies, about forming collective identities. Many traditional forms of participatory culture have embedded values focused around the collective good: go back to the quilting circles and the gifting practices that grew up around them. I don't want to over-romanticize them. As I've already acknowledged, there were structural inequalities in who got to participate. But there was a shared ethic about participation – at least among those they perceived as belonging to "their" community. Networks are more than simply clusters of individuals; they are enterprises formed around shared goals and values; they require us to learn to work together to help others achieve their ambitions, even as we extract value from the community towards our own ends.

Mimi: Social media can be used in individualistic and narcissistic ways, but I question whether the tools themselves determine a value set. It gets back to what we were talking about earlier – that, for me, participatory culture is defined by shared culture, practice, and purpose and isn't simply about a toolset or a platform. So, when we are in the mode of promoting a particular set of values, or participatory culture, I don't think it is about promoting social media or a particular platform. I think Twitter can be used for very individualized and egocentric purposes, but I've also seen it as a tool for collective action.

We can't blame the tools, only ourselves for not taking them up in ways that conform to our values. It's the values of the folks creating the tools, which get embedded in the design, as well as the values of the folks who take up the tools that determine the broader societal outcomes.

danah: I don't think that technology forces people to be individualistic, but I do think that many of the major social media sites are designed for and expect people to be individualistically minded. Groups and collaboration often form a secondary feature, an afterthought. People can indeed use these tools to galvanize others, but the defaults are still egocentric. And the rhetoric and norms among the tools' creators are generally about empowering individuals.

Henry: For me, there's something paradoxical or even oxymoronic about the concept of "networked individualism," even though I understand the critique that certain kinds of social networking platforms encourage the emergence of egocentric networks, especially when compared to older forms of online communities. One of the reasons I am drawn towards the work of Pierre Levy (1999) on collective intelligence is that he's found a balance, I think, between communalism and individualism that makes sense for a networked society. He's essentially arguing that every person needs to develop their own voice and expertise so that they can contribute to the shared production of knowledge and culture.

Levy rejects the idea that a more collective culture requires a hive-mind mentality – forcing everyone to think the same way and know the same things (not that hives actually work that way!). Quite the opposite: he argues that diversity is a central value within a knowledge community – the more diverse the contributions, the richer the solutions the community will develop around common problems and concerns. So, there is a strong focus on exploring personal passions and developing individual expertise, but there's also a strong focus on identifying shared goals and developing an ethical framework based on sharing what you know with others, valuing diversity, and taking ownership over the quality of information you spread. The result is a balance between the individual and the community, between "personalization" and "socialization," which can be difficult in practice, but which represents a meaningful set of goals to work towards within any given group.

Mimi: This whole issue of opposing the individual to a collective is a uniquely Western preoccupation that gets in the way of productive conversations about social change. As someone who identifies culturally as more Japanese, I never really understood why the fulfillment of the collective is thought of as a sacrifice of the individual or individuality. Aren't we fundamentally social beings who thrive when our communities and people we care about and connect with thrive as well? How can we possibly succeed as individuals without contributing to shared culture and goals? Doesn't systemic reform require collective commitment?

We are living through an interesting moment when there's a whole host of trends that are pushing people cross-culturally to recognize concepts like hive mind and network intelligence – that the individual and the collective are inseparable. It's even filtering into the US mindset, which has been so committed to seeing individual and collective interests as inherently in conflict. The challenge, though, is that it takes much more than simply pointing out the fact that we are interconnected and are co-constructing culture and society. We need to take seriously the stakes that existing collectives have in holding onto existing sources of power and difference, as well as the defensive and reactionary moves that accompany encounters across boundaries.

Henry: Given what Mimi just said, I return to my idea that we should be talking about steps "towards a more participatory culture." We have made significant progress over the past two decades in terms of developing new social and technological structures that can sustain collaboration and support creativity across diverse and dispersed publics. We are developing pedagogical practices that can help individuals and groups to acquire the skills they need to participate meaningfully. There is a growing understanding that greater participation in the means of cultural production and circulation are positive values. Yet, the path from here is not going to be easy. There are still many inequalities in terms of access to both technologies and skills; there are still many forces (political and economic) that might seek to contain and commodify the popular desire for participation; there are, as danah notes, aspects of technological design and corporate policy which encourage us to act in individualistic rather than collective ways; and there is much we still do not understand very well about dealing with the diversity of a networked culture.

Chapter 2

Youth Culture, Youth Practices

Introduction by danah boyd

Today's youth are often assumed to be technically sophisticated as a simple byproduct of their birth. Little consideration is given to the diversity of how these supposed "digital natives" experience technology. This language, alongside the broader notion of "generations," obscures the nuances of youth participation. While young people are not the only ones using new technologies, mobile and social media have allowed teens to connect with one another in unprecedented ways. This is particularly notable given increasing limits on their mobility and agency. As teens have embraced social media, both parents and journalists have started to use generational rhetoric to describe – and dismiss – young people's technology use. By positioning youth as "other," adults fail to recognize or appreciate the ways in which youth use technology to connect with others, learn, and participate in public life. Meanwhile, by lumping all youth into a generational category and seeing technology through trend lines, adults fail to see the diversity of youth practices that emerge. The differences between how various populations of youth use technology are as important to understand as the differences between youth and their elders.

Youth culture, as we currently think about it, is a modern concept. The term "adolescence" emerged in the late 1800s, when psychologist G. Stanley Hall wanted to demarcate the transitional stage between childhood and adulthood (Hall 1908). His efforts had political consequences, positioning an age group in a specific class based on their state of mind rather than the state of their physical body. Hall was very aware of the political dimensions of his work and attentive to the efforts by moral reformers to use the notion of "adolescence" to call for the need to protect those who were formerly understood as "young adults" from the demands of the labor force. This drove the eradication of child labor, as well as the emergence of compulsory high school and the rise of youth culture.

In the late 1940s, as many parts of the globe were struggling to recover from World War II, American businesses began to see an opportunity. Parents whose children had come of age during the war and the Great Depression wanted to make up for wartime deprivations and give their children what had been previously inaccessible (Savage 2007). Thus was born the notion of a "teenager," a marketing term used by businesses to target a subset of youth who were still primarily at home with their parents (Hine 1999).

Throughout the twentieth century, ideas about youth culture and the practices of youth continued to evolve, but what stayed consistent was the notion that an age cohort of people could be segregated from the rest of society for either economic or social purposes. Many assumptions were projected onto youth, often by journalists and politicians, who relished any opportunity to depict youth as either rebels and troublemakers or innocent and vulnerable. Twentieth-century parents were simultaneously afraid of and afraid for youth (Valentine 2004). Nowhere was this more visible than through society's attitude towards the media practices of youth.

Although moral panics pre-date conversations about teenagers, youth became the focus of most mid- to late twentieth-century moral panics (Springhall 1998). Drugs, sex, and music were seen as problematic youth vices, but media consumption was often implicated as well. Whether comic books were morally corruptive or video games made kids violent mattered less than the ability to drive fear through the heart of parents by suggesting that any new media would ruin their children.

It is within this context that we must grapple with how young people engage with the internet and new technologies writ large. So much is projected onto youth that it is often difficult to discuss what they are doing, and why, without observation being obscured by ideas of what they *should* or *shouldn't* be doing. Youth are rarely seen as deserving any agency and, yet, they are also judged based on what they choose to do. It quickly becomes a lose–lose situation, justifying restrictions and paternalism.

Part of what we collectively struggle with in this book is the need to unpack what people think about youth and technology versus what we are able to see through our research. Unlike many other topics discussed here, people think that they know something about youth either because they were once young or because they are parents to a young person. And, indeed, each of us – myself, Mimi, and Henry – has a history of how we got into this topic and a process by which we came to terms with the need to separate our own experiences from the experiences of those youth with whom we engage for research purposes.

In my study of youth participation in social media I wanted to understand what everyday teen life looked like once technology was commonplace (boyd 2014). I was a part of the first cohort of youth to have access to the internet as a teenager. At the same time, my experiences online were very much shaped by the types of people who were part of early internet culture – self-identified geeks, freaks, and queers. Given that I was all three, I fit right in. And yet, when I returned to examine teen practices in my early twenties, it was quickly apparent that the geeky internet that I knew and loved was not the same one environment that the majority of youth were experiencing.

I made an analytic decision to study mainstream American teen practices, in part because they were so foreign to me. In my personal life, my hobbies and interests have long dominated my attention to friends, and I have always been terrible at figuring out how to belong, let alone how to be cool. Thus, I knew that trying to make sense of everyday teen practices would not be an act of trying to relive or reimagine my own teenage years; studying mainstream practices functioned as an anthropological exercise from the beginning. Yet, I often struggled with adults who dismissed my efforts as being biased because I was younger than them, even as teenagers regularly told me that I was old. It was this awkward position as a scholar that forced me to step back and examine the historical context in which today's youth are understood.

As we each struggle to understand the relationship between technology, youth practices, and youth culture, we are all forced to grapple with our own position as scholars, parents, and former youth. Our efforts to communicate what we see are further complicated by others' desires to claim expertise based on their vantage point. As scholars, we know that our perspectives are incomplete and we work diligently to address gaps in knowledge, but we also regularly struggle with others' outright rejection of what we see analytically because this information doesn't resonate with their personal experiences, assumptions, or fears. More than anything, this communicative challenge shapes our ongoing effort to make our work around youth accessible to broader publics. We are defenders of and advocates for youth, but many adults do not believe that youth are anything but innocent and vulnerable children. Thus, our decision to tell their story is often activist in nature, even if heretical to some.

Social Media and Young People's Push for Autonomy

Henry: danah suggests we each have our own trajectories into this topic. I was born and raised in a pre-digital era. I worked my way through my undergraduate degree by filing punch cards for a mainframe computer, so I fit the profile of the "digital immigrant," a term I find problematic for many reasons. My own focus on youth and new media came from two sources. First, I was a father who was watching my son come of age alongside the dramatic growth and domestication of digital technologies. I watched him grapple with social issues with his peers online and see how badly his teachers frequently responded to, failed to see, and often sought to protect him from what we now see as the educational benefits of connected learning. For example, I watched the school librarian struggle to enforce a policy which allowed students to use "educational software" during their lunch breaks but not "games," and thus fail to identify how games might foster creative learning. When I was visiting schools, I would ask what kinds of net access they allowed students, and the first wave of responses were often defensive, viewing the internet more as a problem to be controlled than as a resource to be deployed. My son's teachers and principal, at what was a progressive private school, struggled with how much they should allow youth an autonomous space of free expression online and to what degree they should police what occurred there for liability reasons.

Second, I also served as a housemaster for an MIT dormitory, one noted for its diverse forms of subcultural expression (from goths to gamers, but above all geeks). From this place, I could see the first wave of young people who had enjoyed extensive access to digital technologies, observing the ways they were incorporating these tools and practices into all different dimensions of their life and work. Both of these vantages points helped me to recognize the ways that many adults were shutting down opportunities that were meaningful for young people, often out of a moral panic response to technological and cultural change.

Mimi: I sit between danah and Henry in the timeline of technology adoption. My first memories of networked culture were in my high-school years, sitting in my brother's bedroom with his Apple II and acoustic coupler modem, dialing into the pre-internet BBS scene. We were among the handful of kids in an adult-dominated BBS culture. Technology was a way to gain unprecedented kinds of access to adult worlds and power. My brother Joi started his first tech company as a teen, helped set up the first commercial ISP in Japan, and is now director of the MIT Media Lab. I have never identified as a geek myself, but, having grown up with and married into the geek scene, it's always been both foreign and close to home. In graduate school, I met my husband Scott Fisher, a pioneer in virtual and augmented reality. I would never have become an ethnographer of digital and networked culture without these relationships and the opportunity to have close friends and family as key informants. I've been a fond but critical observer of networked and digital culture ever since those early years of playing video games and logging onto BBS forums with Joi. Now that I'm a parent of two teens, I continue to enjoy my close-but-not-quite status.

Colored by my formative experiences with technology, I've been fascinated by how young geeks have been at the forefront of defining not only new technologies but new cultural forms and social practices. At first my focus was on the more stereotypical leading edge of digital culture – gamers and fans – but I've increasingly tried to look at a more diverse range of youth innovation. For example, when I started my postdoctoral work in Tokyo, it was at the beginning of the massive wave of mobile text and visual communication, led by teenage girls. Although I had initially gone to Tokyo to study gaming culture, I added a study on girls' mobile phone culture so I could look at girl-led tech innovation. Now my team is immersed in understanding the proliferating range of youth affinity groups online, ranging from knitters to professional wrestling fans, many of which are culturally quite distant from the early geek online communities.

I try not to be completely blind to the dark sides of youth culture and practices, but I value their idealism, enthusiasm, and creativity. Without idealizing youth, it's important to shine a light on how adults often unreasonably curtail young people's freedom and voice. I see promise in how technology provides openings for young people to shape society and culture despite their lack of economic and institutional power and resources.

Henry: When we are discussing the early subcultural uses of digital media, we are focusing largely on the kinds of culture this first generation of digital youth helped to create for themselves. The young people who most urgently needed alternative channels of social connection and personal expression were those who were least well served by current institutional practices. Let's face it, public schools (and, to a large degree, private schools) are deeply destructive for kids that are different, especially geek kids, queer kids, and kids who come from cultural and racial backgrounds different from the others around them. You are required by law to be there every day, yet you are often subjected to bullying, your social life is organized by principles of exclusion and humiliation, and you often cannot find others who share your passions or interests. I recall my own high-school years in terms of experiences of isolation, alienation, and loss of dignity. My hope was that the online world might allow young people to find others who share their interests without the constraints of geographic location. I certainly saw this phenomenon with my own son, who, when he found himself feeling isolated from the peer culture at his school, sought out friends through interest-driven communities online. He was maintaining an online romantic relationship with a girl living in Nebraska whom he met through a World Wrestling Entertainment chatroom, and he had an important friendship with another young woman who lived in Australia.

danah: My experience as a teenager was very similar. I saw the internet as my saving grace precisely because it allowed me to escape the town I grew up in and connect with people around the world. Some of my most formative experiences are with strangers that I met online – strangers who helped me grapple with my sexuality, strangers who helped me understand politics more generally. Like many who grew up during that period, I imagined that widespread use of the internet would mean that everyone who got online would have such transformative experiences. And yet, one of the things that was most striking to me in my early fieldwork was realizing that most youth who go online do not look to escape their home context.

Henry: Many young people continue to use social media today as a way to connect to some kind of larger community beyond their schools and local community. Liana Gamber Thompson (2012) has been interviewing young people who are affiliated with the US Liberty movement and, in some cases, the Libertarian Party for our Media, Activism, and Participatory Politics project, which is seeking to map different organizations and networks that have been particularly effective at getting youth involved in political and civic life. While there has been a growth in Libertarian values among the current generation, many of these young people do not know anyone else in their school who thinks the way they do, and many of them lack the transportation and other resources physically to go to places where Libertarians meet face to face. Many of them describe the experience of finding other Libertarians online and realizing they were not "crazy." Obviously, over time, all youth – the popular kids as well as the outcasts – have gravitated towards the online world, but some functions of social media are still more apt to be explored by those who are outside dominant structures, while others are simply extensions of the norms of high-school culture more generally.

Coming of Age in a Networked Age

Henry: I often hear people claim that the internet was the first communication technology that young people were able to grasp before their parents, and this is simply not true. The Amateur Press Association in the nineteenth century was dominated by people in their teens or early twenties. The early amateur radio movement in the early twentieth century had strong youth involvement. Radio stations were started by scout troops, for example. There are cartoons during the period showing adults sweating as they try to answer their children's questions about radio, and, when the Federal Communications Commission sought to restrict amateur access to the airwaves, they justified the choice because "boys in short pants" were alleged to have abused the technology to pull pranks on adults. Science fiction fandom was started largely by men in their teens, who published the first zines, organized the first conventions, and eventually became the first generation of professional science fiction writers, agents, and publishers. Young people were drawn to these grassroots media practices because they were seeking a space outside of adult supervision, outside of the constraints of their local community, where they could find others who saw the world the same way they did. This is not a "natural" phe-nomenon; we have to understand it in relation to the constraints on young people's lives, but young people have almost always been the early adopters of new communication practices and have often had to defend the communities they created for themselves against adult attempts at regulation or intrusion. This is often what fuels the cycles of moral panic that surround the introduction of any new expressive medium.

Mimi: Age is one of the most naturalized forms of oppression that we have. It's cross cultural and the least questioned among our struc-tural forms of oppression like race, class, and gender. The ongoing generational tension and moral panics are indicative of how resilient these fault lines are. Ever since we started segregating young people in these age-delimited ways, they've gotten good at finding ways to push back at their elders.

With the advent of electronic media, the modern-day boundaries that protected youth from adult worlds are eroding. Joshua Meyrowitz's (1985) work looks at how television gave children new kinds of visibility into adult worlds and how big a shift that was culturally. Today's social and mobile media are part of this longer trajectory of media and tech-nology, giving young people tools to access and participate in adult worlds and having adult-like autonomy and privacy. It's not surprising that we're seeing a lot of generational tensions around these new forms of social media, because they're reconfiguring the contract about what we thought was appropriate visibility and public behavior for young people.

Henry: Meyrowitz is talking about the loss of childhood in terms of the ways that television grants youth access to what was once exclusively adult knowledge and experiences. He worries that this premature knowledge will destroy childhood innocence or damage children's respect for their elders. You see adults looking foolish on sitcoms, fighting in dramas. Meyrowitz argues that this premature exposure to adult knowledge damages the sense of security young people have within their family. But the opposite is also true. While digital and mobile technologies have created more autonomous zones, they've also ensured that the social lives of youth are more visible to parents than ever before. Various forms of adult surveillance over young people's online lives get read as "good parenting." Adults are supposed to monitor what their sons and daughters are doing online, and, as a consequence, they find themselves witnessing aspects of the socialization process that would be closed to their view were they occurring face to face rather than through mediated communication. Adults historically could not monitor what children did down by the playground, what they talked about when they walked to school, what they said to each other at the mall, or what they did on their dates, but Facebook opens up all of these aspects of kids' lives to potential scrutiny by their parents, their teachers, and other adults. This is the reverse of what Meyrowitz described: adults now get to observe what youth are doing when adults are not around.

danah: Meyrowitz's arguments also hinted at how adults could see youth practices in new ways. I think of this in terms of "visibility" or the ability to see into the lives of other people. When coupled with a culture where parental surveillance is normative, the opportunity to leverage visibility to keep tabs on youth practices can be quite powerful. Of course, visibility cuts in many ways. Just as parents can see into the lives of their children, youth can see into each other's lives and the lives of people that they don't know. Through social media, people have the ability to see – and interact with – people who are radically different than them. This means that youth can be exposed to new ideas and new people, not just in the abstract but through direct interaction. Some see this as a good thing, but plenty of parents do not want their children to be exposed to or interact with children who aren't raised in the same way. The level of control parents are seeking to have over their children's lives has ratcheted up alongside the development of new media.

Even at the local level, visibility can complicate interpersonal interactions. Because interacting through technology often leaves traces, parents sometimes witness interactions out of context and panic. A tiff between friends gets interpreted as bullying or the metaphorical use of a song lyric is taken literally. Concerned parents, determined to protect their children from harm, often go into overdrive, failing to see how misinterpretations amplify their fears. They often respond with restrictions that can limit opportunities, undermine trust, and result in other unintended outcomes. So much is projected onto youth – hopes and dreams, fears and anxieties. And there are so many conflicting messages. As Gill Valentine (2004) argues, people are afraid of and afraid for youth. What emerges are countless myths about teens and technology, many of which boil down to fears about safety, sexuality, and agency.

Gender, Fear, and Moral Panics

Mimi: Studies have shown that the rhetoric around social media is qualitatively different when it applies to girls versus boys. With boys it's about the violence and the video games and the nasty things that they're going to do, and with girls it's about protecting them from people on the internet (Cassell and Cramer 2008).

danah: In my fieldwork, I've consistently witnessed gendered rhetoric around issues such as online safety, but Eszter Hargittai and I conducted a study that doesn't confirm the rhetoric (boyd and Hargittai 2013). We have nationally representative survey data which suggests that a child's gender is not the most salient factor affecting parental concern. Among parents of children ages ten to fourteen, those with girls are significantly more concerned that their daughter will meet a stranger who will harm them and somewhat more concerned that she will be exposed to violent content than parents of boys are. But a child's sex plays no role in shaping parental concerns regarding exposure to pornography, being bullied, or being a bully. When we held for other factors, the sex of the parent also didn't seem to matter as much as other factors such as race. Race is a very significant predictor of parental concern. These findings surprised us precisely because we hear gendered rhetoric all the time, but I've come to believe that what's at stake is probably much more complicated than I thought.

Henry: That is challenging data, danah, since so much of our analysis rests on the assumption that gender matters greatly when discussing the dynamics of family life. What E. Anthony Rotundo (1994) calls "boy culture," the process of peer-based masculine socialization, used to take place outside of the home and was structured around boys escaping the control and supervision of their mothers (at least in the wake of the industrial revolution, which separated the home from the workplace). But, now, this process has been domesticated. Moms are now observing the nasty business of turning boys into men, because it is taking place in their living rooms, often played out on their television or computer monitors, as young boys work through their aggressions or establish their status through video games. Video games make young boys' fantasy lives visible, and mothers feel they have to do something to regulate or correct it. In many ways, what's happening on screen is what earlier generations of boys (myself among them) used to draw in crayons on notebook paper or what we did in the woods at the end of the block. But, now, adults have a much clearer picture of what's going on and are attempting to shape it in ways my parents' generation could not have done.

You may be right, danah, that gender matters more for some concerns than others. We are increasingly recognizing that bullying occurs in both masculine and feminine culture, and, as pornography becomes more widely available, both boys and girls are encountering it in ways that make everyone uncomfortable (Livingstone 2009).

Mimi: It makes sense that gender matters to some concerns more than others, which is consistent with danah's survey results as well as with the range of qualitative studies that have examined these issues. A common tendency is to look at the regulation of media as a solution to these broader societal problems, whether it is violence, challenges to parental authority, or unsavory dimensions of peer culture. I wish people would not go first to whether technology is good or bad and, rather, start with the behavior and consider the different factors that contribute to it.

danah: Many parents I've met genuinely believe that youth today are more at risk than in previous generations because of technology. They have a distorted understanding of sexual predation and think that the internet introduces unprecedented risks of victimization, even though crimes against children have been on the decline since the introduction of the internet, and even though the overwhelming majority of children who are abused are harmed by relatives or people that they know from offline life (see Schrock and boyd 2008). Of course, the mere thought of a stranger harming their child sends chills through any parent.

Perhaps a better example of how adults scapegoat technology is the moral panic around cyber-bullying and other forms of meanness and cruelty in mediated environments (boyd 2014; Bazelon 2013). For better or worse, studies regularly show that no increase or decrease in bullying is associated with the internet (Levy et al. 2012). When surveyed, youth consistently report that bullying happens more frequently at school, with greater intensity, and with more social and emotional costs. Parents, on the other hand, focus on the digital realm. This goes back to the issue of visibility. If a child comes home with a black eye, a parent knows that there was a fight at school, but a grumpy child doesn't necessarily suggest that a bullying incident occurred. Online, where countless interactions leave traces, parents often jump to conclusions about what they see. Unfortunately, our society does not have a strong record in combating bullying – online or off. As a result, parents often want to "solve" the problem by making it less visible – by restricting children's access to social media or pushing for companies to scan for negative content. But this doesn't actually curtail bullying. It is only a Band-Aid on the fear.

Youth in Private and Public Life

danah: What fascinates me is that the battle over meanness and cruelty is taking place during a period in which youth are increasingly encoding their content, rendering some of the most extensive dramas invisible or difficult to interpret. For example, I was sitting in North Carolina with Serena looking at her Facebook profile when I saw two posts that piqued my interest. One said, "She's such a bitch," and was liked by fifty people, while the other said, "I'm sick and tired of all of this," and was liked by thirty-two people. I asked Serena what this was about and she launched into a detailed explanation about the drama unfolding between these two girls over a boy (Marwick and boyd 2014a). These messages were visible enough to draw attention but vague enough only to leave concern in the minds of adults.

Over the last decade, my ability to decode what teens write online has declined, and not just because I'm getting older. With parents embracing social media, teens have developed sophisticated techniques for being private in public. They use song lyrics, pronouns, and in-jokes to have conversations that can technically be accessed but whose meaning is rendered invisible. My collaborator Alice Marwick and I talk about this in terms of "social steganography," or an act of hiding in plain sight (Marwick and boyd 2014b). At one level, none of this is new. Teens have long used song lyrics to express their emotions, and they've used encoding techniques to evade surveillance from snooping parents. Still, it's amazing to see the strategies teens develop to participate in public while maintaining a sense of privacy.

Mimi: One reason young people have led in the adoption of mobile and social media is because they're given so few opportunities for private conversation and for control of their social lives (Ito and Okabe 2005). These new technologies have intersected with that life stage in a particularly explosive combination. We grown-ups tend to have more control of our space and our privacy; we're not subject to the kinds of social controls that kids experience at home and at school, and we've been a bit slower to adopt technologies that give us more pervasive access to private and networked communication.

danah: Technology adoption can be strongly connected to youth agency, but much of social media hasn't simply been about having the opportunity for private conversations, but also about having the ability to participate meaningfully in public life. Over the last few decades, we've seen a significant decline in young people's access to physical public places as well as limitations on their privacy due to ongoing adult surveillance, and so we see youth trying to create spaces where they can be in public as well as more intimate places where they can hang out with their friends. These two often get intertwined, with teens using social media both to participate in public life and to create an intimate space to hang out with friends. They want to be *in* public, but that doesn't mean that they always want to *be* public. This is where privacy and public life aren't necessary contradictory.

Mimi: Social media may have changed young people's relationships to public life, but, when mobile phones came along, the ability to have a private conversation was revolutionary for young kids. Before the advent of a mobile phone, when you called somebody, there was a high likelihood that a parent or sibling would answer. In other words, the adults in your life had some oversight of all your communications. Mobile phones were revolutionary, and teens led adoption because it was the first time that young people had ubiquitous private access to their peers (Ito, Okabe, and Matsuda 2005). Similarly, social media were led by youth because of those unique conditions that youth experience.

At the same time, social media are being adopted by all age groups, just as we've seen with text messaging. So there's a transcendence of the cohort and the life stage to encompass other age groups. I don't think it's the case that kids will necessarily outgrow social media when they become adults. We do see a certain drop-off in technology use when kids gain autonomy. They have professional responsibilities. Youth often retire from fan culture when they get real jobs, for example. We also see a decline in text messaging, especially when couples start living together, versus when living apart. That's an example of life-stage effects. At the same time, I think that the kinds of innovations that young people adopt often foreshadow how other people in other age groups will use the technology – as we saw with text messaging and Facebook.

danah: Many journalists and entrepreneurs see the widespread youth adoption patterns that you're talking about as predictive of technology adoption writ large, but, even when youth adopt a service en masse, it doesn't mean that what they're doing there is at all indicative of how that tool will be used when taken up by non-youth. Sometimes, youth are early adopters of technologies that become widespread, particularly communication technologies. But, when their adoption practices are more deeply connected to their life stage, they are poor indicators of broader practices. I see youth less as a proxy for broader practices and more as an example of how constraints configure practices. For better or worse, the typical American teenager's life is heavily structured and scripted. Teens' lives are overwhelmingly organized around school, home, activities, friends, media, and, to a lesser degree, love interests, religious activities, and after-school jobs. Their movement is bounded and their opportunities to interact are limited. I've found that technology among youth is often employed as a relief valve, enabling them to feel some sense of freedom and power even when their physical bodies and movement are regulated. Their desire to engage in public life, coupled with their limited opportunities to do so, often erupts in fascinating ways. Out of frustration, they often help create *networked publics* – public spaces that exist because of networked technologies and networks of people that help instantiate an imagined community (Varnelis 2008; boyd 2014). Through networked publics, teens express themselves and assert control over their lives. Of course, this often brings them back to the perennial battle between teens and parents for control. This is one of the reasons why examining youth practices provides insight into social resilience.

The Myth of the Digital Native

Mimi: Young people have developed strategies to deal with the conditions of surveillance they encounter vis-à-vis adults in their lives, while at the same time participating more and more in public settings online that have a wide mix of ages. The baseline platforms like text messaging and social network sites can be used in very age-segregated ways. On the other hand, many interest-centered groups are highly mixed as far as age. I see eleven- and twelve-year-olds in gaming communities, and there's little distinction between them and thirty-year-olds. These pockets feel like the internet during its early years, which was dominated by young adults but often mixed in age. There are contradictory effects: some kids take on adult-like autonomy and relationships very early, and other kids use technology to define a very teen-centric space. And the same teens who may be fine participating with people their parents' age on a gaming site would not want to be linked on a social network site with their parents or other adult relatives. Despite the belief that young people are "digital natives," I wonder how much of the distinctiveness of youth behavior has to do more with the unique social conditions that limit their autonomy than with some innate developmental imperative or generational identity.

danah: Digital native rhetoric reinforces generational differences in ways that simultaneously celebrate and pathologize youth. I'm fascinated by the ways in which adults use this language to imply that being "native" is a more illustrious position. As Genevieve Bell has noted, the natives never win. They have historically gotten enslaved, killed, or "harmonized" by powerful "immigrants" (a.k.a. colonizers). Sadly, I sometimes fear that this is a more accurate portrait of how we treat young people's online activities.

Henry: The myth of the digital immigrant generally gets framed in the opposite way: immigrants don't belong; they will never fully assimilate into the digital world; they will never engage with digital media as effectively as their children will. We'd never accept these assumptions today if you were talking about actual immigrants. We'd never accept the premise that immigrants bring nothing of value with them from the old world as they enter the new. So, even if we don't want to reverse the terms, we clearly need to add some more nuance to them. As danah suggests here, both "immigrant" and "native" are incredibly loaded metaphors, and both come with a history of marginalization and unequal distribution of power.

For some adults, the phrase "digital immigrant" functions as a kind of learned helplessness: "I shouldn't be expected to learn how to use this new technology because I wasn't born in the right generation." Yet, senior citizens form one of the groups that moved most aggressively into a networked culture; they have used the internet in innovative ways that support their own needs and lifestyles. Seniors use Facebook to trade pictures, to have more regular contact with their grandchildren, to escape the social isolation of being housebound. They also play online games and buy more music online than young people do.

It's not about age, ultimately. It's about a refusal to participate. Some adults take a passive perspective: "I don't know what these kids are doing. I hope it's okay. I'm not going to touch that part of their life and therefore I have no accountability for it." Some take an aggressive stance: "I can't use this, so you shouldn't either." The latter group of adults can feel deeply threatened by the unknown world, by activities and platforms that were not part of their own growing-up experience. The digital immigrant/digital native language allows adults to let themselves off the hook for making the transition the rest of society has undergone.

Obviously, those gaps in internet usage have filled over time. I don't think middle-aged people lag that far behind the general population in use of digital technology at this point, but they were slower than people at either end of the spectrum to embrace online experiences.

danah: It saddens me how often adults use their status as "immigrants" to justify non-participation, as though they're too old to learn. In opposition, youth are positioned as actively engaged in participatory culture just because they're young. Yet, their position as "natives" also suggests that they're being enacted on, rather than functioning as an agented cohort making active choices to engage. I think that the issue of agency is central to the dynamic of participatory culture and is really missing from the "natives" frame.

Eszter Hargittai (2010) argues that, when we employ the language of "digital natives," we fail to recognize the development of skills necessary to be engaged in participatory culture. She holds that most youth are actually digitally naïve. Their willingness to experiment is notable, but they have limited media literacy, computational skills, or technical fluency. They're assumed to be capable of manipulating technology because they actively text and use Facebook, but their ability to construct a search query or interpret the results is often limited.

Henry: "Digital natives, digital immigrants," how do I loathe ye? Let me count the ways! These terms imply a fixed relationship in how these two generations relate to each other through technology. It assumes a world where the realms of children/youth and adults are absolutely separate, rather than one where they interact with each other in a networked culture in ways very distinct from their hierarchical relationships within schools, families, or churches.

The Risky Business of Youth Practices

danah: One of the consequences of the safety rhetoric is that it creates the generational divides that frame the "digital divide." The message that teens receive is that all adults are scary and dangerous, which means that youth are discouraged from interacting with adults online, even if the goal is to obtain health information or collaborate on educational tasks. Young people who are engaging in subcultural practices like fan fiction are breaking down generational boundaries even as these boundaries are getting broadly reinforced outside of participatory culture. Those who can escape the stranger-danger rhetoric and other rhetoric that reproduces generational divides find that interacting with adults enables them to learn a whole new set of skills, technical and otherwise, that result from intergenerational interaction. But, much to my chagrin, the majority of youth are consistently siloed into communities where intergenerational learning is taboo and talking with adults is seen as inherently risky or dangerous. These youth are losing key opportunities.

Henry: There are spaces where adults and youth have extremely healthy cross-generational interactions. Take, for example, the "beta reading" process within the fan fiction community, discussed at length by Rebecca W. Black (2008). Here, fans read each other's work, offering advice for improvement. Such mentoring practices are built into many of the most popular fan fiction sites. In *Convergence Culture* (Jenkins 2006), I discussed how Flourish, then age fourteen, was giving writing advice to fans twice her age or more, but also learning from adults who shared her passions for Harry Potter. This is not at all unusual within fandom, where people are valued based on what they can contribute, and youth often gain status based on their skills and abilities. Young Potter fans help adults better understand the world of the child characters, and adults help the youth grasp the concerns of the teachers. Even this is too simple a way to describe the collaborations that take place in this space.

Carrie James (2009) has researched structures of digital mentoring and found that relatively few youth have access to adults who can give them meaningful advice about their online lives and help them think through issues of ethics or safety. Lynn Scofield Clark's book *The Parent App* (2012) reaches a similar conclusion. Clark found many different patterns of parental response to digital media, but relatively few of them result in constructive or open dialogues that enable youth to turn to adults for help in dealing with problems they encounter. Our response at the school level has been to declare certain social media or participatory culture practices off limits, to ban use of Facebook or YouTube, rather than to provide trained adults who can offer guidance in how to use social media safely, creatively, constructively, and ethically. There are complex reasons for this: some such limits are required via federal policies, some are a consequence of limited resources and poorly trained teachers, and some represent a defensive posture adopted by educators who have felt parental pressures inflamed via media sensationalism, moral panics, and culture wars. It is hard to see how young people are safer if they have to deal with social media on their own without knowledgeable adults to turn to. Young people do not need adults snooping over their shoulders, but they do need people who can help watch their backs.

Mimi: What we see within so much of the mainstream messaging around media is that the role of adults is to monitor, regulate, and limit. The mark of good parenting in that historic middle-class narrative is all about saying "no" as the proper parental stance (Seiter 1995; Hoover, Clark, and Alters 2003; Livingstone 2002). This works against what you've been describing, Henry, as intergenerational mentorship. It also feeds into this idea of the digital immigrant. That in turn ties to a demonization of the World of Warcraft dad or the Facebook-obsessed mom. These are inappropriate subject positions for parents to take in that more traditional narrative. One challenge to this existing narrative is the emerging image of the geek or creative-class parent who is gaming with their kids, is tech-savvy, and provides a meaningful mentorship that values an empowered identity in relation to new media. This alternative orientation is defining a new digital learning elite characterized by particular kinds of social and cultural capital. For most kids, though, it's more about just negotiating enough autonomy to use social media and text messaging, not about jumping into these much more interest-driven and intergenerational spaces.

danah: This is part of why I am so passionate about youth having access to networked publics. It's only through interacting in and helping create meaningful publics that people can understand society as a whole. I get especially frustrated when adults lament young people's lack of engagement with political life. How can we expect youth to be a part of political publics when we alienate them from public life? I think of engagement in broader publics as cultural training wheels, and I think it's essential to enable young people to explore and take risks and try to make sense of a world beyond them and their classmates. But my passion for this seems almost heretical in certain communities.

Mimi: We have to reassert some important dimensions of the teen developmental narrative that get buried when we focus too much on protecting youth from exploration and risks. We've set up a trajectory for young people that includes a period of their lives when they're experimenting with social identities and new forms of participation. It's a critical period of identity formation. Not that grown-ups don't do identity formation too, but there is a salience to a period when young people have the space to make forays into developing a public identity. Sonia Livingstone, Leslie Haddon, and Anke Gorzig (2012) have stressed that risks and opportunities are often integrally related, and young people can't reap most of the benefits of online participation without being exposed to some degree of risk. As danah already noted, the risks of interacting with new people are generally lower online than in real life, and in that sense the online world can be both safer and more beneficial at providing a start in public participation.

danah: Learning requires failure; there are often bumps and bruises along the way. When people talk about creating a "safe" internet, there's an implication that it's possible to protect youth from every negative experience. While there are certainly some who would love to lock teenagers in a padded room until they're eighteen, this would constitute torture. Teenagers need opportunities to learn how to interact in a healthy way in public and with strangers. They need to learn to take measured risks and face the consequences of their decisions.

I also find it ironic that we fear risky behavior around issues of online safety while rewarding it – even fetishizing it – in other contexts. We relish youth's risk taking when it comes to their openness to innovation, their entrepreneurship, or their willingness to risk their lives as soldiers when they turn eighteen, but we often think that paternalism is needed when their risks do not align with societal values or take place in a medium that we don't understand. It's important to call into question and challenge our assumptions about risk. All too often, brain research is used to suggest that teenagers are constitutionally incapable of having a rational thought. Even if we take brain science as the frame, the brain develops through interaction, experience, and iteration. Protectionism undermines youth's ability to develop healthy responses to risks. This doesn't mean that we should throw teenagers into shark-infested waters to see if they can survive but, rather, we do need to provide training wheels and learn to let go and encourage freedom. Learning and development are life-long processes. There's no magic that happens on a child's thirteenth birthday or a teenager's eighteenth. One does not become Yoda simply by becoming old. Rather than seeing development as an age-based activity, we need to recognize the ways in which it is socially constructed and dependent on opportunities to learn.

Henry: Scholars in the sociology of childhood make a productive distinction between valuing adolescence as a state of being and valuing it as a state of becoming (James and Prout 1997). The developmental model can lead adults to dismiss the cultural lives of youth as meaningful only because of the learning processes involved. Part of what works within healthy participatory culture is that young people can learn to find their own voices in public. They speak out about their own agendas and about making a difference *now*. Those agendas are important in their own right and not simply as a process of identity formation or social experimentation, as steps towards something else. If, as I've argued, the fight for participatory culture should be shaped by the values we place on democracy and diversity, then we should care whether young people are being silenced or whether their voices are amplified through their access to digital media.

Mimi: It's unfortunate that we limit young people's ability to exercise agency, and then lament that they are irresponsible or slackers when they can't step immediately into adult shoes.

I would also point out that we highlight certain negative behaviors as part of the developmental stage of teens, and we can be incredibly unreflective about how adults exhibit these same needs and behaviors. We talk about young people as being obsessively peer-oriented and socially self-conscious without looking at how grown-ups are incredibly status and peer-conscious as well. Now that so many grown-ups are on Facebook and are texting, maybe the idea that young people are somehow pathologically concerned about social connection can be debunked. As social media migrates to other age groups, we are starting to understand how social media orientations that we attached to youth – drama, oversharing, narcissism, attentional fragmentation – are certainly not age specific.

Sharing and Connecting

danah: It saddens me that teens are pigeonholed as the overshare-y cohort who, uniquely, are going to ruin their lives. Are people unaware of mommy bloggers or parenting forums? There's an entire online universe filled with parents documenting every gory detail of their children's lives before they even reach an age at which they can reasonably consent or object to the process. What's going to happen when these children become teens or twenty-somethings whose every poop and burp and childhood antic is documented? And why are people upset when teens share their challenges and struggles while celebrating when adults do the same? At least when teens overshare, they tend to be exposing their own bumps and bruises, not the ones of those around them. And, frankly, teens are often far less revealing in their practices than many adults.

Henry: Would this dismissal of "oversharing" have applied to the consciousness-raising process of the 1960s, when women were talking together outside of the family for the first time about domestic violence, reproductive rights, sexual dissatisfaction, or their desires for greater economic independence from their husbands? These processes of sharing are fundamental to the feminist mantra "the personal is political" and were foundational for the political movements of that era. Something similar could be said about disclosures about the impact of racism on the black community that came out in the churches, beauty parlors, barber shops, and other "hush harbors" (Harris-Lacewell 2006). Or we might talk about "coming out of the closet" as a longstanding tactic in the LGBT community, one which sought to call attention to sexual repression and discrimination in their lives. We deny that same level of political agency when young people are involved in strategic disclosures through social media. We don't assume, when they're talking about their parents, their teachers, and the adult institutions that are imposed on them, that there's an emerging political discourse there. These are tactics of disclosure that allow people to identify and act upon common interests, just as there are disclosures which put them at risk. I am not sure it has ever been a simple matter to distinguish between the two.

Part of what makes disclosures risky in the digital era, as danah has suggested, consists of the ways in which participants lose control of what happens to the disclosed information once it enters into digital circulation. Information moves from "safe spaces" where feminist consciousness-raising occurs and almost immediately enters the view of people who may be much more hostile.

danah: One thing to keep in mind is that the tactics of disclosure can also be valuable tactics of enclosure. Years ago, I remember Angelina Jolie being interviewed on TV about her relationship with Billy Bob Thornton. The journalist was commenting on her tendency to share way too much about her life. Jolie smirked back at the journalist and said something like, "You know, the more that I share, the less you ask about what's really private." This is a sentiment I've heard over and over again from bloggers and others who are quite public online. Sometimes, the more you share, the more you get to maintain true privacy.

Many young people are actively looking to participate in public, but they don't necessarily want to *be* public (Marwick and boyd 2014b). That subtle difference is important because it means that they spend a lot of time making content available, even while the meaning is rendered invisible. So adults complain about youth oversharing, but teens aren't sharing everything. They're making choices – often performative choices intended to entice peers and challenge adults – that allow them to work out how publics work in a networked era. Their innovativeness in this domain gives me tremendous hope.

Mimi: This is another example of how kids are developing innovative and sometimes sophisticated strategies, just like adults are. It's not only older folk who are being reflective and purposeful about their performance in public. Now that Facebook has become multi-generational, I see young people being much more deliberate about how they craft their identities there. Often they build alternative identities on sites like Tumblr or on Twitter as a way of creating firewalls of visibility. We saw this segmentation starting among more geeky kids when we were doing the Digital Youth study, and I feel it is getting more mainstream among youth and also crossing the age divide. The interesting thing about the rise of Twitter was it was not a youth-led adoption cycle, unlike earlier social media. I think the period when youth are this super-special category of early social media adopters might be over. Or maybe things are just getting more segmented and specialized at the platform layer.

danah: We've seen a fragmentation of tools being used, in part because young people are trying to find a place of their own. We're also seeing a movement towards self-expression channels that are more about photos and videos, because they provide a different mechanism for self-expression than previous genres. And, of course, the widespread availability of smartphones helps. We're also seeing fascinating new services pop up that challenge assumptions underpinning social media. For example, Snapchat enables people to take photos and share them in an ephemeral fashion. Adults have responded to Snapchat by flipping out that anything that youth might share through this service must be sexual or inappropriate simply because youth aren't trying to make it persistent. Yet, teens simply see no reason for everything to stick around forever and enjoy the playful nature of this app. I find the adult anxiety around Snapchat fascinating given broader concerns regarding privacy. It highlights the conflicting and hypocritical narratives adults tell about youth. And even when there are teens who are exhibitionists or engaging in risky behaviors, they're not representative of the whole cohort. Teens are not a homogeneous or uniform population. There's huge diversity in what they are trying to achieve, what they really care about, and how they employ what's available to them to get there.

Mimi: It's so important to remember the diversity in how young people take up this technology. That gets erased by the belief that there's some generational zeitgeist which everybody of a certain age is experiencing in the same way. The idea of a digital generation obscures issues of equity and stratification in ways we need to be careful about.

People who tend to be positive about the potential of digital media – and I get implicated in this – are often focused on the more privileged populations. Negative discourses tend to cluster around the behaviors of either more mainstream or less privileged kids. So much of the literature around young people and technology gets framed by the blanket discourse of "Is it good or bad?" because we aren't asking the more fundamental question: "For which kids and communities is it a positive or negative force?"

Henry: We definitely need better pictures of how different groups of young people encounter digital technologies and what kinds of differences those encounters do or do not make in their lives. For example, as part of the Digital Edge project of the Connected Learning Research Network, Andres Lombana Bermudez has been researching the role that digital media plays in the lives of second- and one-and-a-half-generation Latino immigrants living in the Austin area. On the one hand, these young people's use of technology receives much less attention from adults – either positive (in terms of mentorship) or negative (in terms of surveillance) – than that of the kinds of middle-class youth we have been discussing. In many ways, their experience of digital media follows a classic immigrant narrative: they are using these platforms as a means to gain access to shared cultural resources and thus to assimilate more fully into their peer culture, but they are also using them, especially in the family context, to maintain ties to the mother countries they left behind. Because of their greater ESL skills, and because of their greater exposure to American culture and institutions, these youth often end up mentoring their parents in how to use digital tools to achieve their adult goals (ensuring access to governmental and commercial services, tending medical needs, and learning English). On the other hand, these youth have far more limited access to such platforms, given often impoverished family situations, frequently working with out-of-date technologies or enjoying limited access through schools and libraries, which barely allow them time to do their schoolwork, let alone participate in more peer-related interests. While many of the youth Lombana Bermudez has studied are able to kindle real passions and interests in, for example, game design or media production via school and afterschool programs, they lose access to many of these resources, and especially mentorship, as they graduate from high school. They often lack the scaffolding they needed to continue to integrate these interests into their adult lives.

If we are going to make meaningful interventions here, we have to go well beyond the myth of the digital native, which tends to flatten diversity and mask inequality. We need to engage more closely with the very different ways that young people encounter new media in the contexts of lives that are defined around different kinds of expectations and norms, different resources and constraints, from those encountered by youth raised under more privileged circumstances.

danah: Although categorized by age, youth are indeed extraordinarily diverse. Their experiences, desires, interests, and values range so wildly that it's often hard to talk about them meaningfully as one thing. As we try to make sense of youth culture and youth practices – and celebrate the amazing things that youth do – we too must constantly struggle with the easiness of flattening the diversity of youth experience that we know all too well. Finding the language to talk about youth simultaneously holistically and with nuance is nearly impossible, which is why we end up challenging stereotypes, assumptions, and panics more often than projecting a coherent storyline about what youth are. All three of us are committed to making certain that youth are better understood, but we also realize that this is often an uphill battle, particularly because a better understanding of youth requires us to question our adult norms, practices, and cultural values.

Chapter 3

Gaps and Genres in Participation

Introduction by Mimi Ito

As a cultural anthropologist, I've always delighted in seeing the social and cultural diversity of people who take up and reshape new technologies. While we can discern some trends and similarities in how technologies get adopted, I've been focused on understanding how different groups use technologies to fit their specific needs, expectations, and existing institutions. We've already discussed some of the problems associated with assuming a generational or age-based relationship to new technology. This leads us to another question: what are the differences that matter between youth with different experiences and backgrounds?

I grappled with this question early on in my career, during my doctoral research on the uptake of children's software CD-ROMs in the 1990s (Ito 2009). Observing kids playing with these new media in after-school club settings, I noticed how the differences in how young people participated in the club paralleled the differences in media genres of the software. I began to use the term "genre" to describe both media genres and the associated genres of participation in a community. Genres of media in children's software, just as with more traditional media, are ways of framing expectations and categorizing media based on style and other conventions. Riffing on this, I use the term "genres of participation" to describe how the ways in which people engage with media also track along certain styles and conventions. These conventions are embedded in the media but are also enacted through specific contexts of practice, so aren't fully determined by the media genre in play.

Through multi-sited ethnographic study, I identified three different genres of participation and media structured by setting, design, and the market segmentation of the edutainment software: entertainment, academic, and construction. The entertainment genre, exemplified by titles such as Pajama Sam or the Magic School Bus series, centered on playful exploration, with educational references sprinkled in. The academic genre, with titles such as Math Blaster or JumpStart, focused on specific curricular content and a behaviorist approach to learning. SimCity, the title that exemplified the construction genre at the time, empowered the player to tinker and create. The first two genres replicate longstanding genres of children's media, but the third genre was more innovative. It brought the spirit of construction-oriented toys and artistic tools into a media format. While the first generation of multimedia edutainment games included these innovative titles, such as Oregon Trail, Carmen Sandiego, and SimCity, the move to commercial markets was accompanied by hardening into the more established genres. The market came to segment and polarize in a way that tracked to these academic and entertainment genres.

The story of how new innovations get swallowed up by existing structures and institutions is familiar, particularly in high-stakes domains like education. For example, Larry Cuban (1986, 2009) has described, how time and again, the promise of technologies to transform education has withered in the face of entrenched educational practices and institutional imperatives. In some ways, my story of children's software does resemble other stories of agency versus structure, or innovators versus incumbents. However, I do not see a space of freedom, innovation, and agency that is separate from an entrenched societal structure. I view *all* of the actors in these struggles as part of existing cultural genres. When looking at the out-of-school and market-driven learning space, these negotiations also tend to be more fluid than the negotiations around school reform. The innovators in children's software were part of a tradition of progressive education, which stressed a learner-centered and constructivist approach.

Educational technologists Seymour Papert (1993), Yasmin Kafai, and Mitchel Resnick echoed the language of Piaget when they used the term "constructionist" (Kafai and Resnick [1996] 2012) to describe technology-enhanced learning that put the child in the role of programmer and world builder. Even as the children's software industry flowed into existing market categories, structured by the genres of education and entertainment, it was clear that we were seeing the growth of child-centered, hacker-oriented forms of hands-on engagement with software. I saw this in the popularity of the Sims line of products and in my observations at after-school computer clubs. I see the historical popularity of Lego and today's growth of Minecraft as part of the evolution of this genre across technological toolsets. The struggle for institutional acceptance and influence between the genres of entertainment, academics, and construction is ongoing, and new technology can change the balance of power in important ways.

The struggle over genres is a struggle of cultural influence as much as it is one of economic and institutional power. Genres have a conservative dimension to them, and they can be institutionalized and structured in formal ways. At the same time, they are open to evolution and reshaping as part of the process of creative innovation or reinterpretation by audiences, gamers, and users. Unlike social differences that are fixed attributes – like race, class, and gender – genre implies a set of practices and conventions that individuals take up situationally. For example, you could characterize me as an Asian immigrant and a postgraduate-educated, creative-class, middle-aged female. You could then analyze how these characteristics influence my preference for geek culture, Apple products, progressive school choices for my kids, and so on. By contrast, a genre-centered approach would take into account my fixed attributes but also recognize that at different times I might push drill-and-practice software at my kids to get them through a math exam or typing practice, even as I embrace their use of Minecraft as a social and constructive problem-solving environment.

This framework for looking at genres of participation informed the Digital Youth study as well. One of our goals was to understand the diverse ways in which youth were taking up networked and digital technology. We wanted to get beyond blanket proclamations about "kids these days." Our case studies were designed to look at different populations from different vantage points. For example, I focused on the digitally savvy and geeky kids, looking at groups based on shared interests, whereas danah studied peer structures in local contexts such as school. We argued about how things looked different, depending on the entry points and populations. Early on in the work, we started noticing a fault line between the more geeky affinity groups and more mainstream peer cultures in schools. Eventually we identified this split as the difference between interest-driven and friendship-driven participation. This fault line mapped onto the use of technology in interesting ways. In the early to mid-2000s, the friendship-driven practices tended to happen on MySpace and IM. The interest-driven practices were more fragmented but were often taking place on LiveJournal. These genres of participation tracked to online behavior that kids called "hanging out," "messing around," and "geeking out."

Hanging out was associated with friendship-driven learning and participation. It was motivated mostly by social connection and a sense of belonging. Messing around was about kids exploring and experimenting with tools and techniques as part of this everyday social behavior. Dan Perkel's (2008) work on how kids were modifying their MySpace pages is a key example of messing around. He did research on how teens would figure out how to modify profiles and mess with a little bit of HTML. They started to learn some programming skills and sometimes cultivated an interest in digital media production. This is an example of how the social, "hanging out" forms of online participation can become a pathway to more geeky activities. The online world also hands kids new tools for looking around and lurking on forums. There's a low barrier to finding information, so, if they want to know what it takes to modify a photo, or how to install their own memory card, they just Google it. This is behavior that is technically oriented and expertise-oriented, but isn't driven by deep passionate interest or a desire to participate in a geek community.

We found that some kids jump off from this point into finding a new genuine interest. That is the geeking-out part: the fans, gamers, geeks, activists, and creative kids. These kids were driven towards specialized knowledge and getting good at something. They often get held up as poster children for the promise of the digital generation, but in reality they were a small minority compared to the kids who were hanging out. We did find that kids embodied these different genres to different extents, but the skew is towards the more friendship-driven genres. It's important to understand, though, that kids move fluidly between different genres of participation. It's not about categorizing individuals in buckets but about recognizing the palette of available options that the culture hands us (Ito et al. 2010).

It gets more complicated when considering how genres of participation relate to inequity. Although a genre-based analysis does not presume that participation is determined by individual traits or existing forms of stratification, we need to ask whether people engage in these genres in equitable or inequitable ways. For example, the fact that the most geeked-out and constructionist genres skew towards more educated white males is a cause for concern. We need to ask ourselves why it is that girls tend to gravitate towards more friendship-oriented genres and how economic and other factors create barriers and hurdles to participation. Further, what kinds of invitations and exclusions do young people of color experience that are different from those of their white counterparts? In the Digital Youth study as well as my prior work on children's software, it was clear that more production-centered and geeked-out technologies put young people on a path towards technical expertise. In other words, genres of participation are not value-neutral when it comes to issues of equity and opportunity.

Following the Digital Youth project, it was clear that we had to delve further into these issues. Understanding how to expand participation in technologically supported learning environments is key for the network I am chairing. My current research in the Connected Learning Research Network's Leveling Up project consists of case studies of youth affinity groups, which open up opportunity for young people in academic, civic, and career pursuits. For this project, we've selected many cases that have high numbers of girls and black and Latino/ Latina youth. I'll talk more about these case studies and the connected learning model in the next chapter on learning and literacy. When trying to understand how access to opportunity is stratified, it's critical to look at factors such as economics and access to technology but also at the more complex interplay of culture, identity, and affiliation. We are still early in developing a robust understanding of these complicated barriers to participation. While it is easy to understand simple lack of access to technology, understanding how people get excluded from or included in participatory cultures based on their cultural, ethnic, gender, or racial affiliation is much more complex.

Genres and Belonging

Henry: As a media scholar, I have always been intrigued by the use of the term "genre" in Mimi's phrase "genres of participation." Recent work on film and television genres (Altman 1999; Mittell 2004) has moved away from thinking of genres as rigid formulas or sets of fixed textual features. There are no clear borders and boundaries between different genres. Instead, there has been a move towards thinking of genres in terms of interpretive strategies readers bring to their encounters with texts. The same film might be "read as" a western, a melodrama, or a film noir by different groups of viewers, depending on their background, their interests, and, perhaps most importantly, the models of interpretation they can access. We pay attention to different elements, make different meanings, predict different plot developments, depending on which genre we assume is pertinent. Learning to read a genre film is a kind of literacy; access to that literacy is unevenly distributed. I am struck by the parallels between this approach to media texts and the ways Mimi talks about genres of participation here. Not every genre of participation is accessible to every person; not every genre of participation is valued equally by all institutions and their gatekeepers. Some get counted as informal learning; others get dismissed as a waste of time. In both cases sociological or anthropological work must be performed in order to understand how genres operate in relation to other social and cultural institutions.

On the ground, the various communities that grow up around participatory culture often translate these genres of participation into ethical norms and shared practices that are designed to foster greater participation. If you look at pre-digital fandom, there was already a deeply ingrained set of norms that valued what you contributed rather than who you were outside of the community. Within the female fan circles I wrote about in *Textual Poachers* (Jenkins 1992), it was considered rude to ask another fan what they did in their "mundane life." This discretion was shaped by the routine ways that patriarchy devalues women's contributions to the culture. Many of these fans did not identify strongly with their jobs. They were housewives; they were "pink collar workers" – those working in jobs that have been feminized and devalued in our culture, despite requiring a high level of education for access. The attitude was built into the fannish concept of "mundane life," life that lacked deep meanings or passions. This perspective reversed the "get a life" language that people often project onto fans. Instead, these women wanted to be valued within fandom based on what they could do as authors, artists, or critics. The result was an alternative and very fluid conception of status. It is a world where every reader is assumed to be a potential writer, and those who are not creating *now* are assumed not yet to have found the right story to share with the world. When fandom went online, then, these same norms ensured a creative space where young people could be contributors without having to disclose their age. What mattered was their shared experience as fans and their ability to contribute something the community values. This is a great example of how the qualities of participation may be norm-based and not platform-based.

danah: Both of you celebrate the communities that have been formed by people who have used technology to build new connections, learn new skills, and create phenomena that reveal the socio-technical potential of young people engaging with social media. Yet, critics have pointed to how rarified these practices are. Neither geeking out generally nor fandom specifically are mainstream practices. Most young people that I've met aren't even aware of these phenomena, let alone engaged with them, even if they have access to the technologies through which these practices form. There are many genres of participation that are dismissed or viewed with disdain or fear, such as gang organizing or thinspiration remix videos. There are many interpretations of digital content that are viewed as illegitimate. Notably, much of the participation from young people of color and other marginalized youth is often categorized as such, unless it is actively and intentionally framed as productive by adults with societal standing and bounded in particular ways, such as through adult-monitored hip-hop media classes or when activist youth of color use tactics that are recognizable to and respected by older activists.

The Digital Divide and the Participation Gap

danah: Most discussions that struggle with differences in participation begin with the "digital divide," implying that what's at stake is limited access to high-quality tools. There are certainly huge cultural and structural barriers to widespread participation, but there is also the reality that some youth are simply uninterested in participating in the kinds of activities that are often celebrated. I'm more concerned about how, when we talk about genres of participation, scholarly communities often gloss over the issues of what's considered culturally valuable, without recognizing the ways in which stratification and inequity are part of the interpretation of value.

Henry: Throughout the 1990s, the digital divide kept getting discussed as a matter of access to technology. The solution seemed clear, if not easy to achieve: wire the classrooms and libraries and most Americans would have access to networked computing. The latest figures suggest that something like 95 percent of American youth have some access to digital technologies (Zickuhr and Smith 2012). The remaining 5 percent are left out because of deeply intractable problems, such as Native Americans living on some rural reservations that have never gotten telephone lines (Savchuk 2011). Here, there are deep infrastructural problems (not to mention systemic problems) blocking access.

However successful Americans have been at increasing access to the technologies, we have not made as much ground in providing equal opportunities for participation in the kinds of communities and practices being discussed here. In this regard, there are still many being left behind for many different reasons, so there is a need to move beyond talking primarily about access to technology and talk much more about access to skills, experiences, and mentorship. When we wrote our white paper for MacArthur (Jenkins et al. 2007), we used the participation gap as opposed to the digital divide to describe this different, but related, set of issues.

As this term has been taken up by various other scholars and community-based groups, the participation gap actually has many more layers than we first imagined. Those who want to address this problem need to talk about the issue of access to particular kinds of experiences and access to mentorship structures that support and sustain participants' growth and development. We need to describe the sense of self-confidence or empowerment that allows participants to share what they create with a larger public. We need to consider what's required to connect these sites of informal learning to educational institutions, so that what young people learn outside the classroom gets valued in school, leading to further educational opportunities (i.e., higher education) and further economic opportunities (employment, professional development). We also need to think about the political implications of these issues. How might we connect ideals of political participation and civic engagement to other kinds of cultural

participation and social networking? These are just a few of the inequalities that shape who gets to participate and what impact their
participation might have.

We need to devise a more sophisticated vocabulary to describe
these various barriers and to identify strategies to help marginalized
or at-risk youth to overcome the participation gaps. As we do so, we
need to avoid normalizing assumptions that suggest we simply need
to help poor and minority kids to have more access to the things that
middle-class and white youth are doing, rather than exploring diverse
and alternative models for what participatory culture might look like
within these communities.

danah: I don't feel as if we even have a handle on the normalizing
assumptions that have become so central to discussions of participation. There are also tremendous politics at play here, raising significant
issues of power and political might. I will never forget the "aha!"
moment I had when I read "Who's Responsible for the Digital Divide?"
by Dmitry Epstein, Erik Nisbet, and Tarleton Gillespie (2011). They look
at two competing rhetorical moves – the narrative of access that dominated the early discussions and the issue of skills that underpins some
of the participation gaps you describe. They argue that, in policy circles, when people talk about the issue as being one of access, there's an
assumption that the government should be responsible for addressing
the issue. But when there's a rhetorical shift to skills, the onus moves
to the individual or the community to solve their own problem. I find
this particularly fascinating in light of our conversations on a participation gap, because it forces us to think through the kinds of inequities
that emerge or are reinscribed and what should be done to make a
difference. From my vantage point, we're dealing with significant systemic inequality, lack of supportive social networks, and socio-cultural
constraints. These can't be addressed by placing the burden on the
individual. This is why the rhetoric of meritocracy disturbs me and why
I think we need a richer discussion of structural inequity. For better or
worse, access and skills often end up being a distraction when they are
used politically to avoid discussing broader structural issues.

Mimi: Different social groups' relation to technology can change rapidly, but it's much harder to change how those same societal groups are positioned relative to power and resources. We saw this with the recent adoption of social and mobile media by adults and the mainstreaming of gaming. Back in the 1990s, when there was a lot of talk about the digital divide, well-off technical and geek communities had privileged access to computers and the internet. Many assumed that access to technology would give access to privilege when in fact that causality was flowing more decisively in the other direction. The technologies signaled privilege because of the elite nature of the groups who were engaged with it. Now, in the era of the smartphone and networked gaming, access to interactive and networked technology has spread beyond a privileged geek demographic and the digital world is dominated by popular and lowbrow content. If you look at digital media engagement today, it's not stereotypically privileged kids who are doing the most anymore. For example, the Kaiser surveys have shown that black and Latino youth tend to lead in engagement with popular media like television and also digital media like video games. With the turn to mobile digital and networked media, we see these same young people adopting and engaging at higher rates than their white and Asian counterparts (Nielsen 2010; Rideout, Foehr, and Roberts 2010). That doesn't mean that the adoption of new media is leading to a shift in access to opportunity. What it does mean is that we can't pretend that access to digital technology is synonymous with access to elite power.

Race and Class Politics of Participation

Henry: Even so, we are seeing some young people become more politically engaged and develop greater voice and influence through the use of new media platforms and practices, even if those forms of political participation are not fully appreciated by the news media, educators, or political leaders, as we will discuss more fully in the final chapter. We can see these new capacities at play in the struggles around Ferguson and racialized police violence more generally. People have noted that net-based activism reflected the emergence of a new generation of civil rights leaders who were tapping into the power of participatory politics. With each new incident over the past years, the public has been able to respond more quickly and more effectively and direct the attention of the media and political establishment onto situations that could no longer be swept under the rug. These protests represent a visible example of how young people are starting to change politics, especially politics around race, gender, sexuality, and social justice in America.

In the summer of 2012, Cathy Cohen and Joe Kahne (for the MacArthur Foundation's Youth and Participatory Politics research network) released the results of a large-scale national survey of young people, designed to map their use of social media and its connections with their political lives. Their data found relatively few differences across races in terms of the likelihood that young people would use digital media for political purposes. Specifically, 43 percent of white, 41 percent of black, 38 percent of Latino, and 36 percent of Asian-American youth participated in at least one act of participatory politics during the previous twelve months. The racial gap in terms of engaging in participatory politics is much narrower than the gap in voting, where there's a 15 point divide between the most active group – African-Americans – and the least active – Latino/Latina. There are also some signs that those who participate online in political discussions are substantially more likely to vote in the future. My current project – Media, Activism, and Participatory Politics (MAPP) – has been seeking to explore some of the groups that have been most innovative and effective at drawing young people into the political process.

danah: I would never argue that people of color aren't participating in meaningful political resistance, but the kinds of political practices that are made visible and celebrated are almost always those from white, middle- and upper-class communities, just as the kinds of informal learning that get recognized as valuable and used as examples inevitably come from more privileged communities. When we look at the numbers, we see diversity. But when we look at what stories get academic and media attention, we rarely do so. When stories of technologically mediated activism by people of color do emerge, they're often deemed controversial and problematic in ways that do not parallel the treatment of white youths' activism. Or they're dismissed as being just digital without real activist teeth. Why?

Mimi: We do need to do more work in linking the literature on political awareness and mobilization by people of color with the technology world, which is why the work that folks like Craig Watkins (2010) and Cathy Cohen and Joe Kahne, or the cases of DREAM activism (Zimmerman 2012) and Muslim youth (Shresthova 2013) that the MAPP project are undertaking, are so important. If you look beyond our more parochial technology discussions, we see a robust recognition of the political awareness of oppressed groups in this country, ranging from civil rights activists, to immigrant rights, to Arab and Muslim groups in the post 9/11 era. Many of us would argue that youth who have grown up under conditions of structural oppression and racism tend to have a more sophisticated political awareness than those who have not.

If we believe that today's participatory culture is a site for learning to be digitally literate and net savvy, and can put young people on a path towards more self-directed learning, then I think there might be an interesting story emerging here. Some of the case studies in our Leveling Up project are pointing in these directions. For example, Crystle Martin (2014) has been looking closely at the dynamics of professional wrestling fandoms, which enlist youth from diverse socioeconomic backgrounds. Matt Rafalow and Kiley Larson (2014) have looked at interest in fashion as a site of connected learning. Maybe some of the young people growing up in less economically privileged households are actually being primed for learning in ways that their middle-class counterparts are not. At the same time, youth in professional middle-class families have growing achievement anxiety that is clamping down on their space for autonomy and exploration (Pope 2001; Levine 2006). Clearly, wealthy kids still have many more paths to opportunity than poor and working class kids. At the same time, there may be a unique opportunity to close the participation gap if we can have some well-positioned policies and educational interventions.

danah: But what would it mean to close the participation gap? How do we grapple with the fact that people learn different things through their different experiences? I can't imagine either of you would argue for homogenizing people's experiences. We know that social networks matter and that who you know influences your interests and learning. In a perfect world, we'd all know an equal number of people with diverse perspectives who would expose us to a plethora of new ideas. But this imaginary world doesn't exist. There is no neutral baseline. The notion of truly equal opportunity is a fantasy. I struggle with understanding how it's possible to close the participation gap meaningfully, given that there are going to be both natural and culturally situated differences in experience and exposure. Some activities are going to be more valorized than others because they're more recognizable by those who are privileged and/or powerful.

Addressing the participation gap isn't just about access and skills. Some of the most egregious inequities have a lot to do with people's structural position within a broader network. One of the challenges for me around participatory culture is that even awareness of the kinds of activities in which one can participate is very much shaped by who you know. Being exposed to some of the things that we relish – even awareness of something as simple as fan fiction – requires being connected to certain people. Youth are judged based on the norms of their peer group. And they're also able to imagine possibilities based on the practices of those around them.

Henry: I have been drawn recently to a passage from Jean Lave and Etienne Wenger's early work on "legitimate peripheral participation" (1991: 36): "As a place in which one moves towards more intensive participation, peripherality is an empowering position. As a place in which one is kept from participating more fully – often legitimately, from the broader perspective of society at large – it is a disempowering position." This framing forces us to pay more attention to the scaffolding that different communities provide for moving towards greater participation. It asks us to distinguish between situations where people have not yet acquired the skills and self-confidence needed to participate and situations where there are structural obstacles blocking full and meaningful participation. So, our first task is to seek to identify and eliminate those structural obstacles, making it possible for more and more segments of our society to participate meaningfully. Recognizing that participation can take many different forms, another task is to help identify forms of scaffolding that enable people to move more fluidly from peripherality towards more engaged and empowered positions. Sangita Shresthova (2013), for example, has been tracing the various ways that American Muslim youth have been struggling to find and assert their voices and shape their representations in the wake of 9/11. This is often a one-step forward, one-step back process: given the chilling effects of the racial profiling unleashed in the aftermath of the Boston bombing in April 2013, we saw many that had struggled towards self-representation via social media retreat again.

We might draw a comparison with the concept of the "public sphere." Our theories have moved from a focus on the idea of one big public sphere, where all public opinion is formed, towards a recognition that there are multiple counterpublics, where localized opinion needs to be consolidated before groups are empowered to speak effectively within a more generalized space. There has been recognition, via writers such as Mary L. Gray (2009), that some of these counterpublics may be temporary and precarious, struggling to survive under very adverse conditions. Yet, we still need to better understand the points of contact between these different publics and counterpublics, the ways ideas move (or don't move) from one to another and influence or enable larger conversations between groups that are not yet speaking to each other comfortably. We might think about the relations between different forms of participatory culture in similar terms: there's a need for distinctive practices and spaces, but there should ultimately be a way of getting these populations to speak to each other. What are some of the differences you are observing in your work?

danah: I'm personally intrigued by the kinds of learning that are particular to marginalized groups trying to route around cultural restrictions and institutional barriers. Many middle- and upper-class youth have access to the internet at home via computers, often their own laptops or tablets. As a result, they grumble when their schools ban social media sites, but they don't do much to resist the censorship except to try out a few rumored work-arounds. In less privileged environments, before the widespread adoption of smartphones, I was astonished at how often teens had developed broad strategies for finding new proxies, breaking through censor walls, sharing what they learn, and iterating as they engaged in a game of whack-a-mole with school administrators and government agencies, who theoretically created these restrictions to protect them from themselves and others. Because school was the only place where these youth had significant access to the internet – and because digital media are so central to participation for many of these teens – marginalized youth often went to great lengths to find a way to route around any restriction placed in front of them. As a result, they learned highly sophisticated techniques for navigating the internet in order to get access to forbidden sites and services.

I've also watched less privileged youth surpass mainstream youth because of how they navigate limitations. Consider the rise of the Danger Sidekick in the mid-2000s. It was launched by T-Mobile, which was not a carrier that most middle- to upper-class parents used. Wealthier parents tended to put their children on their phone plan and give them a hand-me-down phone. T-Mobile, which had a pre-pay option – you could pay for each month in the store – launched the Sidekick and targeted urban youth. Early adopters started complaining to customer service about data and usage, so they made the data plan all-you-can-eat. They also decoupled the data plan from the calling plan so that users could choose one or the other.

This combination of options was very appealing to low-income youth from urban regions, who quickly adopted the Sidekick as a text plus data-only device. AOL Instant Messenger (AIM) was on the phone, and teens went wild. I heard rumors that, at the peak of Sidekick's popularity (with only 150K devices), the device was accounting for one-third of AIM's US traffic. These predominantly black and Latino youth were doing fascinating things with their devices before "smartphone" was even a concept.

When the iPhone came out, it was celebrated as the first popular consumer smartphone, even though it was inaccessible to less privileged youth. Sidekick was never really maintained, and its core developers all went to Google to produce Android. But there was an amazing moment in the history of smartphones where low-income young people – and particularly low-income youth of color – were being more innovative and engaging more deeply with the "always-on" life imagined by digital connectivity than any of their wealthier peers.

I think it's helpful to remember when, where, and how marginalized youth end up forging new pathways in order either to achieve parity with their wealthier peers or to address directly their social conditions. At the same time, it's important to recognize how they get shut out of these systems by new innovations meant to curtail their creative acts. The non-generative technology movement that Jonathan Zittrain (2008) critiques doesn't just curtail the actions of geeks; it severely limits what marginalized youth can do. Today, most youth have access to the internet through their phones, but there is very little room for technical creativity in an app world.

Henry: Sasha Costanza-Chock's book on the immigrant rights movement in Los Angeles (2014) tells an interesting story. Many of those who would become digital activists first acquired skills in video production and digital sharing to share pictures and videos with families still in Latin America. They were trying to preserve some continuity of traditions, some sense of social connections. Those production and circulation skills spread across the community. They did not emerge top-down as something taught to youth or bottom-up as something youth discovered on their own. They emerged from traditional family and community life, as young people worked with their parents and grandparents to learn how to use this technology to preserve older ways of life that mattered to them. Young people began using these skills and platforms for political ends, especially in pursuit of educational and citizenship rights for youth who had been raised largely in the United States (Zimmerman 2012).

Mimi: In the Digital Youth project we found it was often the lower-income teens who had more autonomy, ingenuity, and resourcefulness. The ability to solve problems and engage in self-directed learning needs to be cultivated, and that can only happen when young people are given the time and space to explore, as well as have some responsibility. But it's not enough to celebrate the fact that resource-poor communities are using ingenuity and finding work-arounds. The question is how that capacity can elevate opportunity. It's not going to happen just because access to technology and online networks is becoming more pervasive. I don't see the participation gap as resulting from a lack of ingenuity, creativity, or even skills. I see it as resulting from a lack of social connections to opportunity. There have been and will continue to be a ton of low-income youth who are highly engaged, smart, and creative, but the amazing things they are doing will be marginalized without some principled interventions that are targeted squarely to these equity issues.

danah: This gets at the crux of my anxiety when thinking about these issues. Knowledge and skills matter little when you don't have the social connections to open doors to opportunities. I can't help but think of Paul Willis's (1981) study of how working-class kids get working-class jobs. He argues that there is a significant cultural cost involved in transitioning to the middle class that is not typically recognized in popular rhetoric about class mobility. While entering the middle class may provide more financial stability, it is often done at the expense of a person's personal relationships. Leaving one's hometown to go to college or taking a job in a different community can feel like a betrayal, and yet moving is often necessary for upward mobility.

Class mobility has less to do with explicit forms of education and more to do with connections and support. The majority of young people are on some major social media at this point – Facebook, Instagram,

Twitter, etc. – but what they see on their feeds, and thus what becomes normative for them, varies depending on the people in their network. I sit with privileged teens who are being socialized into the norms of elite colleges through their older friends and family, then I watch the feeds of less privileged youth reflect anti-educational agendas. And I get it. I get that those who are written out of many opportunities find self-worth by demeaning certain paths, but this is how local norms get developed and reinforced. So, while I can celebrate how technology opens up new possibilities, I can't help but worry about how it also reinscribes what is normative in ways that are especially costly for less privileged youth.

At the height of MySpace's popularity, I received a phone call from an Ivy League admissions officer. The college was interested in an applicant from South Central Los Angeles. He'd written a compelling essay about leaving behind the gang culture that surrounded him. But the question they asked me was, "Why would he lie to us when we can tell the truth online?" They had gone to his MySpace profile, which was filled with gang insignia. And, rather than reading it as a survival tactic, they read it as proof that he was really a gangbanger himself. This situation highlights how people's class position also shapes how they read others' online activities. Parents and educators often talk about the things that youth should do to make sure that they aren't interpreted in the wrong light, but we rarely put the onus on privileged adults to account for the cultural power of their interpretations.

One of my favorite uses of #hashtag activism addressed the issue of interpretation head-on. After Michael Brown was killed in Ferguson, many youth of color objected to how the teen was portrayed in mainstream media. News stories often used an old picture of Brown seemingly throwing a gang sign rather than using his very recent high-school graduation photo. Youth began posting two images of themselves – one acceptable to white society and one not – to Twitter, along with the hashtag #IfTheyGunnedMeDown, highlighting the biases of media coverage of black and white deaths. In doing so, they reminded the public of the ways in which interpretation is a structural inequity issue.

Mimi: These issues of interpretation and stereotyping run deep. They relate to a whole host of assumptions, including stereotypes about cultural and intellectual deficiencies. I've learned from my colleagues who have researched what Kris Gutiérrez describes as "nondominant" groups such as Latino immigrants. Gutiérrez argues that educational research on students who are not part of the dominant culture, and who are economically marginalized, often assumes cognitive deficiencies and social and cultural deprivation. The discourse is about how immigrant kids can measure up to the benchmarks of the dominant culture rather than recognizing the strong capacities and cultural competencies that these young people and their communities already possess.

Gutiérrez argues for the term "nondominant" rather than terms such as "at risk" or "disadvantaged," which signal this more deprivationist frame (Gutiérrez, Morales, and Martinez 2009). If we can start from a place of valuing the existing capacities of nondominant communities, then the solutions with respect to technology and education look very different than those efforts that try to "fix," "bridge," or fill in for "deficiencies" in nondominant youth. Instead, we would look to new interventions and technologies to support and amplify existing culture, values, and capacities inherent in nondominant settings.

One place to look for alternatives could be in what Juliet Schor has been calling "connected consumption." Her team has been conducting a range of studies on how communities share resources through peer-to-peer markets like time-banking, open learning urban farming, maker spaces, and food swaps as part of the Connected Learning Research Network (Carfagna 2014; Schor and Thompson 2014). These peer markets, as well as some of the community dynamics we see in our Leveling Up cases, give some hints as to how we can go about building social capital within communities rather than taking kids out of their existing social networks. For example, maker spaces and hacker spaces are community-run places where people can have access to tools to create things, find supports for learning, and connect with mentors. There is a growing movement to think of these spaces as intergenerational learning environments. Jeff Sturges has taken this model to Detroit, where there is a lot of expertise in making and manufacturing but also high rates of poverty and unemployment. He is working in a church, together with the pastor, and leveraging local capacity in order to rebuild their community. His maker space has become a place where older folks can come and impart their skills and wisdom to the youth, and everyone is creating and making things in ways that build relationships, elevate the community, and help with local economic viability (www.mtelliottmakerspace.com). That's a fundamentally different approach from trying to build pathways for a select number of kids to become coders or designers in order for them to leave their communities.

I admire the efforts within education that are about opening up traditional pathways to opportunity for kids who don't otherwise have access. We need more black kids in tech, we need more girls in gaming. All of that's important. But it doesn't solve the capacity issue when you're in an era of contracting opportunity. It just reshuffles the deck. Rebalancing the gender and racial dynamics of people at the top is an important agenda, but, at the end of the day, there are only a handful of kids who are going to make it out of poor communities, and you're not going to change the fact that they're leaving the majority behind.

The formal educational system can't fundamentally address equity in an era of contracting opportunity, because the focus is on assessment and sorting kids into existing opportunities. Traditional educational achievement is about managing the competition for existing resources and opportunity. When the pie is expanding, this management gives more people access to opportunity, but when the pie is contracting, it produces more inequity. Today we have to focus on building more capacity, entry points, and pathways to opportunity. I think our work in education has to be pursued within the context of real-life action and communities. Otherwise it becomes just another exercise in sorting and reshuffling.

Social Capital and Networks

Henry: To achieve the kinds of changes you are proposing, Mimi, we need to acknowledge the many invisible barriers to participation that operate within even the most robust forms of participatory culture. People involved in a community's practices may not fully recognize or understand the ways the practices they take for granted may be huge hurdles for someone who is not already involved in that community. I've seen the debate play out at many fan conventions: the community openly embraces diversity, yet they end up with a room full of forty white people asking two or three people of color why there aren't more people like them attending the convention. This turns out – surprise, surprise – to be a largely counterproductive approach to the problem of cultural segregation. This debate erupted online in 2009 via a range of fan discussion lists in what became known as the "#racefail" debate. It started as a conversation about racially insensitive stereotypes in genre fiction, went through a deeply divisive and painful process, but ended up with many fans gaining greater consciousness about the invisible ways that race enters into a participatory culture (Klink 2010).

My own recent thinking on this issue has emphasized the social construction of taste. There's a strong body of research showing how class shapes taste, which is understood as a set of shared social norms within which personalized choices occur. So people raised in different economic or racial/ethnic communities may have different degrees of access to cultural materials or practices. They may be encouraged to define or discouraged from defining their identities in certain ways, may be more or less likely to express certain fantasies or desires, and thus are going to be more or less likely to enter specific communities of practice. Those communities do not need to be actively excluding anyone on the basis of class or race for them to end up with relatively homogeneous memberships. They may be open to anyone who shares their tastes and interests but nevertheless limit meaningful participation to certain groups, simply because the tastes around which fandom organizes are more likely to be found among middle-class Caucasians and Asian-Americans than other segments of the population. Many of these participants may feel they have had to defend their tastes against conservative or anti-intellectual teachers and parents, without realizing they also had more resources and support for doing so than those of other cultural and economic backgrounds.

danah: Participation is so deeply entwined with the people you're surrounded by. It's often destabilizing for people to be exposed to other networks through shared platforms or interests. I've seen tremendous racist and homophobic backlashes when people are exposed to other values on Twitter. I agree that these incidents open people's eyes, but they don't solve the structural problems. Getting people to talk about racial insensitivities doesn't obliterate them. And when people talk about these issues online, they're doing so within their networks. Inequalities are baked into people's social networks.

Henry: Talk is not the same thing as substantive change, but it can be a first step. But we also need to recognize that segregation within subcultural communities is really a symptom of much larger changes in how American society has dealt with diversity. In the aftermath of the civil rights movement, there has been a shift – not everywhere but in many parts of the country – from overt racism (burning crosses) and legalized segregation to a more informal system of social exclusion, which may be well meaning in its goals but is deeply divisive in its effects. People still live largely segregated lives. This, as danah and others (boyd 2011; Watkins 2010) have noted, extends to their online lives. It may well be that people of color who are born into the middle and upper classes, live in integrated communities, adopt a middle-class sensibility, and form bonds within racially mixed classrooms have found their way into some of these sites of participatory culture. They identify strongly with some of the other participants, until something happens that forcefully reminds them of their different cultural histories and trajectories. Those who have remained largely marginalized through class-based factors find it much harder to engage fully in some of these practices.

So, rather than identifying geek culture as something that appeals only to middle-class white kids, we may want to think about what it is about this culture that welcomes some people but excludes others, or at least doesn't pull others into participation. So, what does participation look like in other kinds of spaces that operate according to different racial dynamics? How do we think, for example, about white youth who find themselves drawn into the world of hip-hop? Most of us doing this research come out of geek culture and are drawn towards researching communities that have mattered to ourselves and our children, and we've fought hard for the right to write about them. Yet this focus leaves us blindsided when it comes to dealing with communities that fall outside of our comfort zones. We still know relatively little about the racial dynamics of participatory culture more generally.

Mimi: Getting our arms around these dynamics of inclusion and exclusion in youth interests and affinity is incredibly challenging. Geek and nerd culture is complicated because, while it is tied to academic and technological privilege, it doesn't have high status in youth culture, where interests like music or athletics are more dominant. It's much cooler to be hanging out with friends, engaging in the heterosexual marketplace, and exchanging tokens of popular culture through fashion and music than it is to be nerding out on tech with your teachers. As danah notes, affiliation with working-class culture and networks creates one set of divisions. Some forms of affiliation that possess high status in youth culture but not in adult culture can also produce similar outcomes. One of my big questions coming off the Digital Youth study was "What is the difference between those kids who are engaged primarily in friendship-driven circles and kids whose social lives revolve around interests and causes?" The kids who do engage deeply in civic, creative, or academic interests and who form close bonds with teachers and other adult experts often get marginalized as the nerds, geeks, creative freaks, or whatever the label *du jour* is. Why aren't there more and diverse kinds of genres and social identities that get sanctioned by our learning institutions as smart, engaged, and creative? That's the kind of participation gap that I'm concerned about addressing as an educator.

A lot of my earlier work was really a celebration of geek learning. How do kids get into deep verticals in communities that reinforce expertise and are challenge- and inquiry-driven? How do they develop technical literacy and skills in social networks, in status and reputation-building? We could say the same for other youth affinity groups, like hip-hop or sports fandom, which may not be geek identified but exhibit similar interest-driven learning dynamics. More recently, I've come to the realization that it's not enough that kids are diving into deep verticals. They need to connect that learning to things that matter in terms of broader societal values and achievement that will open doors for them in their adult lives. What we find in a lot of youth subcultural groups is that, if they are defined in opposition to adult cultures of achievement, they can have a counterproductive effect as far as connections to opportunities in adulthood are concerned. This is particularly true for young people who are highly identified with nondominant subcultures that have low social and cultural capital in institutions of power. It reinforces the sort of social inequity that we don't want.

danah: Oddly enough, this makes me think about the significance of 4chan. 4chan is an image board that was started in 2003 by a fifteen-year-old named Chris Poole to share content that he thought other boys his age would find interesting: pornography and anime. This site is often described as the underbelly of the internet, but it has also become ground zero for some of the most innovative cultural productions and youthful political action out there. 4chan has given birth to both popular "memes" such as LOLCats and political action groups such as Anonymous. It's easy to critique many aspects of 4chan, but what's surprising about the formation of this site is that its users aren't necessarily privileged elites. While its culture of anonymity makes it hard actually to discern who is on the site, the content seems to suggest that the crowd is predominantly young, male, and white. But when I started looking for teens who participated in 4chan, I began to notice that, with a few extremely wealthy exceptions, many of them were not particularly wealthy or highly educated. Generally speaking, the youth I met were the kinds of geeks who felt siloed in their home communities but found kinship online through sites like 4chan. But they were more diverse than any one category could easily describe. Biella Coleman (2014) found the same thing when she started to investigate who was beyond Anonymous, one of the most politically oriented offshoots of the site.

Those on 4chan are engaged in all sorts of practices that blur capacity-building and political resistance. The tactics that members of 4chan take include those that are recognized by adults and those that are seen as anarchic and politically dangerous. Participants have been celebrated by the establishment for their ingenuity and arrested as terrorists for their more political acts. Sites like 4chan reveal the complex and interconnected nature of different kinds of participation.

Mimi: At the end of the day, they may be raising awareness, but I doubt for most of the kids that 4chan is a pathway to opportunity, and that's unfortunate. You want to support more young people who can connect and translate between these deeply engaged subcultures and institutionalized sites of power and influence.

This is one of the reasons that in my research network we're not just talking about interest-driven or geek learning, but about connected learning, where social and interest-driven learning is connected to institutions and sites of power and opportunity (Ito et al. 2013). This connection can take many forms. For example, youth can apply capacities of community organizing, writing, or technical skills to what they are doing in school or work settings. They can also leverage relationships with mentors and peers developed through their interests to be introduced to a new opportunity in the workplace, civic life, or education. We also see narratives and frameworks in which young people were immersed through an interest-driven setting to understand something happening in school, as when Civilization or StarCraft helps a young person understand the history of war in class. Which isn't to say that, just like having friends, geek knowledge and subcultural engagement aren't valuable in and of themselves. But we feel it is important to tie informal and peer learning to opportunity as well.

danah: How do you see connected learning opening up opportunities for those who do not have meaningful social networks or supportive family situations? How can connected learning bridge the gap that exists because of structural inequities?

Mimi: The core of connected learning is this understanding that it takes relationships to open up opportunity. That's why the focus is on learning within the context of social engagement and shared purpose, where young people are learning to get things done with both peers and adults. It's not enough to push content and skills at kids, or to say that there's knowledge out there on the internet. If young people don't have relationships with peers and caring adults with whom they identify, and who can build those paths to opportunity, then the content and skills don't do anything for them. I think kids are smart about that too. They are deeply skeptical of programs that might provide training, instruction, or consciousness-raising without being connected to relationships and social networks that are meaningful for them and that are going to support them.

This is the difference between engineering learning within a sequestered classroom environment, where the young person is expected to market those skills on their own in the world outside the classroom, versus a community-based maker space, where a young person is involved in a shared project with peers and adult mentors. These are places where they create things of value to the community and can raise funds to sustain their work. In connected learning, we talk about individual and group outcomes as interconnected, so that the learning environment is about building capacity and high-quality culture and knowledge rather than competing for scarce opportunities. We're arguing against the vision of education as a competitive race in a winner-take-all career market. Instead, we ask what learning can look like if it's about contributing to shared endeavors and building relationships, and not primarily about competing with your peers.

Henry: In that sense, the most powerful forms of participatory culture have always embraced some elements of what you are calling connected learning. For example, when my grandmother participated in the quilting bee, she was bonding with the older women in her town in ways that would support other aspects of her life. The samba schools functioned as a place to plan for carnival, but, in turn, as George Lipsitz (2006) has discussed in relation to the Mardi Gras Indians in New Orleans, they were entering into a culture that, while being "network rich and resource poor," provided a support system during lean times. Science fiction fandom long functioned as a training and recruiting ground for future professionals alongside the work it did as a self-sustaining culture. All of these are traditions where experts and novices, youth and adults, learned side by side and provided support for each other for other aspects of their lives.

danah: When I was a teen, the internet enabled amazing opportunities to build new networks and connect to new people and new ideas that went far beyond what was available to me in my hometown. I was living the bridge between what is now called participatory culture and connected learning. When social media first emerged as a phenomenon that was poised to go mainstream, I was ecstatic, envisioning all of the ways in which young people could enrich their social networks. But this wasn't how it played out. From the get-go, people connected primarily to people they already knew. And then the stranger-danger moral panics emerged, resulting in unbelievable cultural pressure not to engage with strangers (Marwick 2008). Sure, some youth broke out of that rhetorical grip – and many of them are engaged in practices that are at the core of both participatory culture and connected learning. But what frightens me is that, rather than connecting people to shared learning opportunities, the fear-mongering around social media has increased divisiveness.

The lack of diverse personal social networks – and the cultural resistance to strangers – makes me wary about a new participation gap brought on by people's engagement with social media. I think that fear – and those who broker in it – significantly affects the development of both participatory culture and connected learning. The key to equality is to incite young people to engage with new people. Ironically, this is the historical power of two of our largest institutions for youth: the military and college. And, yet, the pervasive discourse in American society is that doing so puts youth at risk. We've started discouraging youth from interacting with new people – a.k.a. strangers – both online and offline. If we don't find ways to enable meaningful cross-cultural network development, the core projects that both of you are passionate about will be undermined by a participation gap driven by a narrowing of networks.

Henry: The challenge you identify here concerns all three of us deeply. On the one hand, the kinds of interest-driven communities that we care about have expanded dramatically since the early days of the Web. More people are participating than ever before. The infrastructure is more robust, the projects deeper than they once were. We now know much more about what makes such participatory communities work. We are seeing research that demonstrates their pedagogical value, and they engender meaningful experiences.

Yet, on the other hand, there might have been a time when we could have seen the growth of participatory culture as a logical progression from the embrace of networked communication, and fewer users than we would have expected have taken that step. Instead they maintain stronger contact with friendship-based networks with which they also interact face to face. In some ways, the commercial growth of the web, especially coupled with the atmosphere of moral panic, has pushed us towards greater privatization – a retreat into our digital enclaves – rather than further experimentation in how we might use these tools to connect with more geographically dispersed communities of interests.

We should have known all along that there was nothing inevitable about how people were going to use this technology – and, of course, on some levels, we did. But those of us who value participatory culture must advocate for it, whether this is challenging the moral panic discourse or making the case for why participatory communities and practices should be connected to educational institutions. Each of us, in our own way, has tackled some dimension of this problem, and this is a project that will continue to demand our collective attention for years to come.

Mimi: I also see strong trends towards the kind of network homophily that danah is concerned about. We saw this when mobile phones were first taking off in Japan in the 1990s. When people have the option to associate primarily with people with whom they are most in tune, they will tend to do so. It's what Misa Matsuda (2005) called the growth of selective sociability. This has been hotly debated in the internet space around issues like the echo chamber (Sunstein 2009) or the filter bubble (Pariser 2011). All of this is not necessarily in conflict with Henry's observation that participatory culture continues to grow. Taken together, it means that social networks and cultural capital are becoming more important as determinants of opportunity. Status and power are negotiated through our formal institutions and organizational roles, but also through these much more fluid networks and practices. Without our public institutions like schools and universities taking on cultural identity and social networks directly, I also fear that we won't see the intergenerational and cross-cultural network development that we need in order to address inequity in participation.

Chapter 4

Learning and Literacy

Introduction by Mimi Ito

Most of my research has focused on how young people engage with new technology and digital culture. As a researcher of education, I've always looked at these practices through the lens of learning and literacy. I've been a bit of a black sheep in the educational research community, because I haven't focused on in-school learning. But I've been in good company with other ethnographers who have focused on learning "in the wild" (Hutchins 1995). This vein of work has also gained legitimacy within educational research over the years. As I was coming of age as a scholar, ethnographic and practice-based approaches to studying learning and literacy began to move from the fringe of the field to become a challenge to the orthodoxy of experimental and psychological approaches. I feel fortunate to have been trained by a brilliant group of educational ethnographers and cognitive scientists while these approaches began to be taken more seriously by the educational establishment. The work that I've been doing as part of the MacArthur Foundation's Digital Media and Learning initiative, developing an approach that we've called "connected learning," is testament to the strength of this research. In coordination with the research, a growing cohort of educators have been developing and refining these ideas in the classroom.

As a graduate student at Stanford I apprenticed at the Institute for Research on Learning (IRL), the Xerox Palo Alto Research Center

(Xerox PARC), and the Laboratory of Comparative Human Cognition (LCHC), all of which were developing new ideas around situated learning and cognition.* It was an exciting time intellectually – we were seeing people in many fields debate and synthesize a new paradigm for theorizing and supporting learning. Educators had believed that learning and cognition happens "in the head" of individuals, and that education should be about getting stuff into those individuals' heads so they can carry knowledge around and apply it in different settings. Researchers at IRL, PARC, and LCHC demonstrated through empirical study that learning is inseparable from the cultural identities, practices, and material settings of everyday life. They argued that the educational agenda should focus not on getting things into kids' heads but on supporting contexts where kids could belong, participate, and contribute.

Jean Lave's *Cognition in Practice* is one of the books that exemplified how this research challenged assumptions about learning. Lave took on one of the most school-identified disciplines – mathematics. She studied how people engaged in mathematical reasoning as part of grocery shopping or cooking at home and contrasted these observations with what happened in classroom. In one oft-cited example, a Weight Watchers participant needs to measure out three-quarters of a two-thirds cup serving of cottage cheese. After muttering about how he should have learned this in school, he said he "got it." He measured out two-thirds of a cup in a measuring cup, then dumped it on the cutting board, patted it into a circle, marked a cross on it, scooped up one quadrant, and served the rest (Lave 1988: 165). Whether it was in measuring ingredients or making price comparisons in a grocery store aisle, Lave found that people who didn't feel they were competent in

---

* This includes the celebrated work of Lave and Wenger (1991) on situated learning, work on situated cognition pioneered by folks like Lucy Suchman (1987), Jim Greeno (1998), and John Seely Brown, Allan Collins, and Paul Duguid (1989), as well as ethnographic approaches to learning that I touched on in chapter 2 (Eckert 1989; Goldman and McDermott 1987; McDermott 1980). Another allied set of frameworks came from the LCHC brand of cultural psychology (Cole 1998) and activity theory (Engeström et al. 1999), which also situated learning within human activity, culture, and history.

school math performed quite well in everyday problem-solving for a meaningful purpose.

Situated learning theory not only took aim at the foundations of cognitive theory, it challenged the core assumptions of our educational practice. Why should we be sitting kids down in rows to learn math in the abstract when it is both more engaging and effective to learn it in the real world or through meaningful social activity? These research studies resonated with those of us who subscribed to progressive education and its hands-on, meaningful, and real-world forms of learning.

This challenge to experimental psychology in education has a counterpart in debates within media studies between socio-cultural theorists and "effects" researchers. Just as educational psychologists study how "content" gets into the heads of students, media effects researchers use similar methodological tools to study how media messages get into the minds of audiences. Shared culture, identity, and practice don't enter into these frameworks. It's not surprising that those of us who critique such approaches talk about participation as an important part of culture and social context. By examining participation we see our relationship to "content" – whether that is educational or entertainment-centered – as part of shared practice and cultural belonging, not as a process of individual "internalization." This is why Henry's notion of participatory culture resonated so much with me when I first encountered it, and why we tend to see similar potential in social media and grassroots media production. These differences also tie in with the evolution of media education. While there is a long-standing approach to media education that focuses on critical analysis of media messages, we see a growing interest in approaches that take a more participatory and production-oriented focus (Buckingham 2003).

New media technology has the possibility to reproduce many of the traditional assumptions of learning: disembodied, behaviorist, and sequestered. Examples include drill-and-practice software and more efficient testing regimes. But I've been captivated by the potential of digital and social media for progressive education through new means. I've marveled at how young people – for example, US anime fans – pick up knowledge and skills by engaging with peers around shared purpose and passion, and how they take up digital tools for new forms of creative production. These fans pick up Japanese, as well as sophisticated writing and technical skills, because of their love of cult media and through practices like fan subtitling and video remix. In these settings, learning is a side effect of creative production, collaboration, and community organizing, not the explicit purpose of the activity. I doubt that those same kids would have learned as much in a formal classroom setting in the quest for a good grade.

The youth who are learning in this way are not typical. You could call them "positive deviants" (Pascale, Sternin, and Sternin 2010) – people who are unusually successful in mobilizing resources widely available in a community or setting. In the Digital Youth study we found that most young people were going online to hang out with friends in ways that were not particularly focused on academic or expertise-oriented learning. A significant number did use online networks to geek out in areas of interest, such as gaming or fandom, and many of these groups were intergenerational in composition. But only a very small handful of resourceful young people were taking their community-based learning and connecting it to in-school, civic, or career-relevant settings. I realized it wasn't enough simply to celebrate the cool things that kids were creating and learning in their affinity networks if we wanted to make these activities matter for education and other forms of opportunity. Most young people needed support from parents, educators, or other caring adults in order to broker connections across settings. This could take the form of a parent who guides their child to a specialized camp or program in their area of interest, an affinity network that actively seeks civic opportunities, or a teacher who sponsors an interest-centered after-school club. In order to better understand these supports, in our current Leveling Up study we are researching affinity networks that connect out to sites of opportunity that are academic, civic, and career-oriented.

Participatory Learning

danah: When we started working together on the Digital Youth project, the goal was to understand how youth were integrating the various new media technologies into their lives for personal, social, and educational purposes. One of the most powerful interventions that came out of this was a realization that there was often a pathway between hanging out, messing around, and geeking out. This led you to work with learning researchers to help envision connected learning. The history that you just offered puts a lot of this in context, but can you explain more explicitly the connected learning piece?

Mimi: The connected learning model that we are developing as part of the Digital Media and Learning initiative focuses on connecting young people's interest and peer-centered learning with academic, civic participation, and career possibilities. The settings that we found were most effective for these connections are guided by a shared purpose, are centered around production, and have an openly networked dimension to them (Ito et al. 2013). A cornerstone of connected learning is also a commitment to equity. Progressive and interest-driven learning has been available to privileged children with access to specialized enrichment activities, but new media offer the potential to make these experiences available to many more young people.

This model grew out of the insights from the Digital Youth study as well as a set of design principles being developed by practitioners and designers in the DML initiative more broadly. The model values a wide range of youth interests as potential entry points to connected learning, so we're not just talking about tech or literature nerds but also looking to interests as varied as popular music, dance, fashion, or skating. It's not necessary for the interest to have a digital focus, but we do see new technologies as a way of lowering the barriers to accessing specialized communities of interests, self-expression, and sharing with a community. It's still early days in developing, refining, and testing the model in practice, but it's exciting to see that it seems to resonate not only with folks who have been part of the DML work but also with a much wider network of researchers, designers, and practitioners.

Henry: We are each making interventions around education that stress collective rather than individualized, personalized, or privatized modes of learning. For me, a participatory learning environment is one that respects and values the contributions of each participant, whether teacher, student, or someone from the outside community. It's one where members have some degree of control over their own learning process and some input into collective decision-making. Such classrooms are hard to achieve in practice, in part because fewer and fewer of the decisions impacting learning are being made at the most local levels, as teachers are forced more and more into a standardized curriculum in support of regimes of standardized testing. Teachers feel as if they have limited control over what happens in their classrooms; parents feel as if they have little control over what gets taught their children; and students feel as if they have no control over what or how they are taught.

The more authoritative a classroom structure becomes, the less students feel that their own voice and their own choices matter, the less free they are to pursue their own passions and interests, and the less likely the curriculum is to reflect the realities of their lives beyond the schoolroom. A participatory classroom, on the other hand, would be one where students help to shape the curriculum, define the norms of what constitutes appropriate conduct, and feel free to share what they know with others in their own community. For those who are used to a teacher-controlled classroom, this shift towards power-sharing can be frightening.

Mimi: The idea of participatory learning creates a useful bridge between socio-cultural forms of learning theory and media studies, but the term has never really worked for me. I have a pretty strong theoretical commitment to recognizing that all learning is socially situated, and it has been a big fight in our field to have that recognized to be the case – whether that is classroom learning or out-of-school learning. I was trained by classroom ethnographers who documented in excruciating detail how students and teachers interactionally co-constructed the learning environment, culture, and practice. Young people are never passive vessels in even the most traditional classroom setting. I think signaling "participatory learning" as something unique sets us back in that progress we've made in the learning sciences at this theoretical level, though I don't have any beef with the elaborated description of what Henry means by the term "participatory learning." I am much more comfortable with the term "connected learning" to describe the aspirational learning environment.

Henry: If I had known the term "connected learning" when we started doing our work, I might have adopted it. But let me try to defend my term. While all forms of education exist in some kind of social context and all people perform some roles in supporting those learning spaces, it is not hard to imagine a series of choices which would centralize much of the authority on the teacher or the school system, give learners limited roles in deciding the materials covered, actively discourage participation in discussion, and focus more on rote learning than activity-based or constructionist learning – all decisions which would result in a less participatory model of education. As long as we are talking about public education, there are constraints on how participatory learning can become, since teachers cannot escape certain legal obligations stemming from their roles as agents of the state, restricting how much control they could shift towards the students. As a consequence, just as all education is participatory to some degree, all education in a public-school context is also authoritarian to a degree. So, we introduced the concept of participatory learning as a way of modeling for educators how they could make choices that might allow students to learn by participating within a classroom that took on many of the traits of a participatory culture. We did have an emphasis on bridging from school to the student's life world, but the work of Mimi and her collaborators on the Connected Learning Research Network have really focused so much more attention on this aspect of reimagining the learning environment.

Mimi: We're facing a big challenge, which is that today's networked world requires a different set of skills, literacies, and social relationships in order to thrive and succeed. Much of the focus of the twentieth-century educational system is out of step with what we need today to navigate this changing ecosystem of how information, culture, and knowledge are produced and circulated. Henry, the white paper that you and your team put out on twenty-first-century media education (Jenkins et al. 2007) set up a lot of the terms of the debate that we've been having in subsequent years about how best to support young people in learning to thrive in a digital culture.

Henry: One of our primary goals for the white paper was to try to identify, specifically, the core social skills and competencies that young people might need to acquire if they were going to participate meaningfully in the kind of networked society we've described throughout this conversation. For one thing, this new focus requires a movement from thinking of literacy as a personal or individualized skill to thinking about it as a skill that has to do with how we relate to others in our community, thinking about how we create, circulate, collaborate, and connect with other people. Howard Rheingold, in *Net Smart* (2012), claims that network literacy is a fundamental part of being able to manage our lives and our knowledge today in a competent manner. By that, he means both the most technical notion of how a network works and the ability to understand and meet the norms of a networked community – how to put information into circulation. Too often, in today's schools, a student's writing ends up on the teacher's desk and sits there waiting a grade. Rather, we should think about literacy as involving the capacity to engage with networked publics, to share what you write, and to receive feedback from some kind of larger community. In that sense, we were trying to move literacy from the capacity to produce and consume information to the capacity to participate in some larger social system. This expanded conception of literacy brings new kinds of ethical expectations – a greater sense of accountability for the information we produce and share with others given the impact of our communication practices on the people around us.

Information Overload?

danah: The average digitally connected person has more access to more information today than ever before in history. It's not remotely possible for anyone to consume all of what is available. According to YouTube's statistics page (www.youtube.com/yt/press/statistics. html), more than 100 hours of video are uploaded to the site each minute. Today's media-rich ecosystem isn't just full of highly edited content produced by professionals or experts; everyday people produce it, sometimes for a public audience and sometimes just for their friends. People are swimming in a wide array of different types of information: news articles, status updates from friends, tweets from celebrities, informative blog posts, funny animated GIFs on Tumblr, etc. Sorting out what to consume is not an easy task. This prompts a sense of "information overload."

For some, solving "information overload" tends to focus on how to deal with massive amounts of information. This thread tends to take on a narrative of optimization. Technologists love to discuss tools that make people more efficient at consuming more information. Other people debate the issue of multitasking or accepting the onslaught. Commentators like Linda Stone (n.d.) argue that there is no such thing as multitasking: there is only continuous partial attention, and it's physiologically and socially costly. Some debate the importance of accepting the onslaught of information. Computer scientist Michael Bernstein uses the phrase "Twitter Zen" to describe his practice of dipping into social media without worrying about what he's missed, because, as entrepreneur Caterina Fake (2011) points out, "fear of missing out" (or FOMO) drives obsessive social media practices.

Another debate underlying these issues has to do with information quality. In a world where there is so much information, how much of it is credible? How does one find and prioritize "good" information? And what does it mean that the internet enables access to inaccurate, incendiary, and outright hateful information?

There are many pragmatic and political considerations at play when thinking about the massive quantity of information available today. What does it mean to be literate in an environment where information isn't just at your fingertips but flooding your senses? Should we expect people to develop sensibilities to make informed judgments about what they see, or should information be vetted and controlled in order to limit people's exposure to questionable content? And what does this mean vis-à-vis vulnerable populations who may be more susceptible to being manipulated by content driven by an agenda?

Mimi: We're at an interesting moment where there is a lot of public debate about whether these technologies are good or bad for kids, for learning, and for culture. Many critics have said that we can't focus anymore and we can't have reflective thought. It's valuable to have critiques, but at the same time I think it's important not to lose sight of the fact that information abundance is a good thing. Social connection is a good thing. When young people get grief for being online too much or not going to the library, they just give you a blank look and say, "But the internet is awesome. I can look up anything. And it's really easy. I like to be in touch with people I want to be in touch with." It's important to keep the big picture in view. Given that we have these incredible new opportunities for learning and knowledge and social connection, how can we optimize them and what are the things we need to be careful about? What new practices of mindfulness, awareness, and restraint do we need to cultivate? This is why I feel so strongly that it's not enough to have a research agenda that is about describing and critiquing but also to have an educational agenda that is about supporting productive forms of engagement and literacy. Otherwise critique ends up being more about building the reputation of the researcher than being part of solutions.

It reminds me of when, for us as a species, calorie abundance (as opposed to calorie scarcity) became a problem. We had to learn new skills in order to manage the fact that fats and sugars are abundant and cheap in our diet, and there are definitely downsides in terms of our health that have resulted from it. We see a similar concern with negative effects of information abundance, but that doesn't mean that we want to go back to a diet of starvation in terms of communication and information.

Henry: There's a dangerous tendency to talk about these experiences of media change and information overload as if this had never happened before. We might productively go and look at the turn of the twentieth century, when an explosion of mass media was impacting American life, urban areas were experiencing the introduction of electric lights, signs and billboards cluttered the landscape for the first time, millions were moving from the farm to the city, blacks were moving from the South to the North, and waves of immigrants were bringing new peoples to America. Progressive-era writers described people as overwhelmed by information, unable to keep pace with the changes. There were so many signs and so much noise and so much to take in. People talked about sensory overload; about the challenges of dealing with diversity in the lower east side of New York, where people from all over the world were being shoved against each other and having to sort out their differences; about innocents from the farm not knowing how to deal with the sensual temptations of urban nightlife.

If you were a Brahmin in Boston in the late nineteenth century, this was all deeply, deeply threatening because it could destroy your way of life and strip away your historic privileges. These elites had exercised a monopoly over knowledge and culture; they got to determine what counted and what didn't count in their society, and that power was under threat. If, on the other hand, you were an immigrant or part of the rising middle class, there was enormous gain in having access to greater information and greater cultural diversity. So we always have to ask who gains and who loses? What's at stake? What are the risks? What are the benefits?

The interesting thing is we survived all of this. Human beings adapted to new cultural experiences, they lived through the transition, they developed social structures that helped them deal with the risks and the dangers, and, yes, elite power reasserted itself, regaining some of the privilege it felt was on the verge of being lost. People didn't reach this point without some pain, without some negative consequences, and some of these problems persist, but the process was not as devastating or dramatic as reformers of that era had feared. So we have to start with an assumption that we'll survive the transition and we'll identify the structures that we need to cope with the changes that are taking place around us. We do need to be offering an affirmative picture of a society that is concerned with the welfare of all, embraces diversity, identifies and promotes shared ethical norms, supports the forms of civility required for democratic debates, commits to mutual responsibility over the kinds of information we circulate, and helps to ensure broader access. If we're going to talk seriously about participatory culture, we have to figure out what these new structures of knowledge and social interaction should look like and find ways to transmit those skills and values to the society at large.

danah: I think it's important not just to think about an increased availability of information but also about what information manages to get traction and why. I'm fascinated by what information spreads and who gets attention in a mediated world. Who has the power to make certain that their perspective is heard above the fray? In a world where, theoretically, anyone can participate, who actually gets to control the public narrative? While I appreciate the historic reminders of empowerment of less privileged populations, I'm not convinced that this is what's happening. But it's also not so simple as to say that privilege is simply reasserting itself.

Politicians celebrate when they get a million followers on Twitter, but I follow teenagers whose tweets are read by millions. Activists who try to get a message to be spread far and wide often fail, but when a teen posts something sexual or grotesque, embarrassing or shocking, it often spreads at an obscene speed. Those who accept a market-driven world often shrug at this disparity and say that people get what they want. But I think that there are serious consequences to the attention economy. What captures people's attention is often the most salacious, fearful, and gossipy content available. It's the junk food of content. And there are plenty of folks out there preying on people's gluttonous media practices. I realize one interpretation of this is that social media democratizes participation, but is this really what we mean or even want?

Managing Media Consumption

Mimi: One problem I have with some of the criticism is that the response is to reel things back into old systems of legitimacy, control, and validation: to say no to technology, go back to reading books, and shut off Wi-Fi in the classroom. Just telling kids to disconnect or hoping technology will go away is not realistic or even desirable. The technology is infinitely malleable, and the question we need to be asking is how new norms, practices, and literacies can make our engagements most productive individually and collectively. It's not a simple binary. We're starting to devolve power away from institutions to collectives and individuals and networks, and that means that every person has to take responsibility for the credibility of information, their ownership and production of it, in ways that weren't quite as necessary in an earlier era.

danah: Even information is often boiled down to an assessment of whether a particular piece of media content – or a particular platform – is good or bad. Teenagers tell me that they've been told that Wikipedia is bad while Google is good. When I push them on this, I find that they're often not sure exactly what this means. But they've been taught to read certain platforms as trustworthy and to eschew others, with no critical apparatus to understand why. I'm saddened by the low level of computational and media literacy out there and the broad refusal to engage with these issues. It's easier to be afraid of technology and media than to engage critically with it.

Much of what's at stake has to do with the ways in which norms and values are negotiated in our networked society and how we reach widespread consensus when there are significant value-laden conflicts. Whose values get to shape public discourse? How do we think about personal desires versus societal benefits? When information and tools reflect values, how are they interpreted or rejected?

Henry: There's been a tendency behind many of these platforms to assume that what the majority likes is what's best. This majoritarian logic means that there is very little if any commitment to ensuring that we have access to a diversity of perspectives, rather than simply allowing the most hegemonic thinking to be reproduced yet again. These sites do not necessarily create mechanisms which ensure that minority tastes and interests are fully represented, any more than broadcast media has done so. And, so, one area where we need to develop more critical literacy is around the mechanisms and processes that determine our relative access to different kinds of materials. As we confront today's complex problems, we need to expand as much as possible the range of solutions that are proposed and the different kinds of expertise we tap. But most of us do not yet have very good tools or skills for seeking out and sustaining this diversity of perspective.

It's one thing to look at the highest-circulating videos, which tend a bit towards the lowest common denominator – or at least appeal to majority tastes. It's another to look at those videos that are reaching a few thousand or even a few hundred thousand people; at that level, they tend to reflect minority tastes and perspectives, or at least niche interests. Many of those videos share ideas that would never have gotten wider circulation under the broadcast paradigm, and they are making a difference in the lives of the people who produce and share them. This is the heart of the expanded communication capacity we are discussing. But there are limits in terms of the ability of many of these videos to break out from their niches and reach a more mainstream public. These are ideas that are still blocked from becoming part of the larger cultural and political agenda. So, here we go from a notion of information overload back to one of information scarcity. As long as we have this illusion of plentitude, we are discouraged from asking what is missing from the conversation.

danah: Niche communities are phenomenal, but there's an increasing tendency to turn everyone into a niche community, especially given the fetishization of personalization. This can be both beneficial and problematic. On the one hand, niche communities and marginalized individuals might relish the opportunity to have content and information tailored to their interests. On the other, what does it mean when our information society gets so fractured that people have no common ground? Algorithms that are designed to tailor content for individual people have significant cultural implications. They can be empowering and make unexpected voices heard, but they can also result in fragmentation and massive localization. Much of this depends on how these systems are architected, with what goals in mind. I think of Tarleton Gillespie's (2014) work on the politics of algorithms and platforms. How do certain values get baked into systems? What should we do when we see conflicting values and norms? Does it behoove us to challenge people's views because it's for the greater good, or should we be focused on giving people what they want most?

Media Effects and Media Ethics

Mimi: Now that more of us are not only media consumers but producers and distributors as well, how media shapes society and culture is our collective responsibility. I don't think we are there yet, but we need to be moving away from the frame of what "they the media" are doing to us to what "we the media" are responsible for. In working with young people, it can be challenging to move them from a subjectivity of a media consumer to that of a producer. It is even more challenging to support the cultivation of a mindset of social responsibility about the sharing and circulation of media. When we work with kids who have had limited access to digital tools and networks, it's not difficult for them to pick up skills in media creation. The bigger challenge is for them to take a leap to being an active contributor to the online world and develop an identity as someone who has real contributions to make.

For example, my team worked with Jonathan Worth, who for years has been teaching an open online photography-based digital storytelling course – Phonar – with college students. We co-developed Phonar

Nation, a version of the course tailored for teens, which relied exclusively on photo capture and sharing on mobile devices. Lower-income teens we worked with loved taking photos and creating stories, but getting them to share online was a challenge because they didn't see their work as "good enough." When they did get their first feedback from others on the open internet, you could see them light up. The next big step is to encourage reciprocity and to have them comment and give feedback on others' work. That's when you start to see them cultivate a subjectivity of someone who has influence in shaping online culture and media. This is the subjectivity that we see with kids who are highly engaged in affinity groups and networked culture, and it is a critical component of developing both media literacy and media ethics. When they can move even further, and begin to look under the hood at the technical conditions of media production and circulation, that is yet another step.

danah: Media literacy in a networked era isn't just about making sense of images, text, and other content that is produced by people. All too often, we forget about technical creations that produce cultural artifacts with significant implications. A few years ago, communication scholar Mike Ananny (2011) was downloading Grindr on his Android when he noticed that the app store recommended that he next download a "Sex Offender Search" app. There are many different possible explanations for how that recommendation was made, so Mike wrote an essay in *The Atlantic* to ask critical questions about this recommendation algorithm. His technical fluency allowed him to critically interrogate the feedback that he received from services, but many people have little to no understanding of how technical systems work. I've met so many teens who think that Google hand picks what appears at the top of a search query or who think that Facebook manually curates what goes into their news feed. Media literacy in a technical world isn't just about trying to understand the content that you see; it's also about how it gets there in the first place. If you don't understand how the most ubiquitous algorithms work, you're more likely to be duped.

Information is power. It can be empowering, but it can also be a tool for disempowerment and manipulation. For example, I'm very curious about the future of neuro-marketing and efforts to use personal data to understand and control people. These are very nascent technologies, but corporations are increasingly turning to them in an effort to manipulate the public in order to capture people's attention or capitalize on their emotional responses. They use statistical models to determine which messages are most effective in terms of neuro-biological responses or which presentations will produce the highest number of clicks. These technologies are often introduced to undermine people's critical awareness of how they're being targeted and manipulated through the messages and media narratives around them. We've seen this script before with propaganda and the early work of Bernays ([1928] 2005).

Henry: danah, I am struggling with your focus on manipulation here. I agree that you are raising an area of enormous concern, but I'm having trouble separating out your claims from broader debates about media effects (more as they operate in the realm of public policy than as a paradigm of academic research). There's such a persistent desire out there to imagine that media is affecting us on some visceral level that's beyond our control and outside the realm of the rational. These arguments dismiss the degree of control people have over media, the ways in which we assert that authority on a routine basis – that emphasis on agency is at the heart of my arguments about participatory culture.

danah: I share your skepticism with media effects because the approach that gets categorized under that name tends to lack nuance. All too often, correlation gets associated with causation, particularly when the analysis is covered by news media. There are a lot of cultural issues at play in terms of how we consume media and integrate it into our lives. It's equally unhelpful to presume that every interaction with media is cultural and none of it is biological or neurological. I think that disciplinary siloing ends up doing us a disservice, and that those of us who tend to take a cultural stance on these issues need to take seriously the possibility that there are cognitive processes at work too.

Neural pathways get formed through exposure to information and experiences with situations. This enables learning but also makes possible manipulation. I think that we need to develop techniques and approaches for critically interrogating the kinds of practices that are emerging in the world of marketing, including those that assume more data equals more knowledge and that the answer to humanity can be found in neuroscience. We can eschew these mythical frames, but I think that dismissing statistically oriented and biologically oriented approaches is limiting. I would really like to see interdisciplinary scholars work together to construct a more critical approach. There's too little understanding of how biology and cultural influences intersect. The interplay between both is crucial for making certain that people have the critical skills needed to interrogate the manipulation that they are experiencing.

For example, we know that Fox News differentially lights guests based on their perspective. Does this affect how people perceive those guests? How? Can we help the audience be more aware of this form of manipulation? We know that sounds are used in media to signal emotional responses to specific ads or content. Can viewers be attuned to these subtle influences? How do we help them be aware?

Henry: The disproportionate status ascribed to science in our culture makes such a collaborative perspective difficult to imagine. There are a massive number of people who take assertions made about "brain science" uncritically, who believe that this research has pushed much further than it has, and there's a tendency for people in those fields to make claims about culture that are value-laden while using their authority as "scientists" to mystify the ideological values underlying their work. Such claims are accepted in court proceedings or government hearings on very different terms from claims made from a more humanistic vantage point. So the problem is not getting humanists to be more receptive of biological arguments, but to create a space where cultural arguments get taken seriously by people in power.

Leaving these methodological disputes aside, we are at a moment where issues of media literacy – and media transparency – are coming to a head. On the one hand, there's probably more access to information about how media is produced today than at any moment in the past in terms of all the director's commentaries and making of documentaries on DVDs. We've turned the critical analysis of how media gets produced into its own kind of popular entertainment. Everyday people are surprisingly aware now of the choices that go into, say, the development of special effects or the design of costumes or the framing of shots. Unfortunately, most of that information is not produced with skepticism about the ideological effects. You are unlikely to learn anything about manipulation through a director's commentary on a DVD.

On the other hand, we've had decades of US educators calling for media literacy classes and largely failing, whereas in many other parts of the world there are requirements in support of media literacy that have varying degrees of success. As those struggles have continued, some media literacy advocates have become embittered and sometimes moved from skepticism towards cynicism. Their version of media literacy has too strong a focus on manipulation, to the point that young people are often seen as victims of the media rather than as potentially active, creative contributors to the new media landscape.

Beyond either of these models, we have a growing number of people, especially young people, who have everyday experiences as media-makers. People are learning from each other, often in informal ways, how to produce media. As they make media, they have to make ethical choices about what kinds of stories they want to tell. And they are looking more and more at the media they consume through the eyes of someone who is actually or at least potentially a media producer.

Mimi: In his work on media education, David Buckingham (2003) describes the difference between an inoculation approach and a production-centered approach. That protective inoculation approach is important but not sufficient for today's media ecology, because young people are media-makers. They're circulators. They're curators themselves. The inoculation approach was developed during the reign of commercial media, before today's ecosystem of social and amateur media. Our educational challenge is much more complex because we have to deal with that longstanding, more traditional left-leaning issue of critiquing commercial media agendas, as well as with issues like digital citizenship and what it means to be a good participant in media culture. Being critical of powerful media producers does not make you a responsible participant in participatory culture. Media literacy may not even be the right term for it. Our mindset has to start moving beyond "How can I protect myself from media corporations?" and towards "How can I contribute in an effective and responsible way?"

danah: I also think it's too simplistic to view the corporations or big media as the sole manipulators. Many of the same tools that we're seeing corporations use are also being used by everyday people to capture the attention of their friends and followers. Few are as sophisticated as professional media-makers, but many are engaged in amateur practices that parallel what we see among experts, such as video hoaxes. People manipulate each other, consciously and unconsciously, for all sorts of reasons, including attention and entertainment.

I don't think that inoculation or abstinence helps people cope with the contemporary media ecosystem. From my perspective, people are most critically aware when they understand how media is produced. This is one of the reasons that I've long subscribed to the commitments of both of you to getting people engaged in the production side of media. People learn a lot about media when they can see it from both sides. Being an integrated part of the media landscape is actually an essential part of learning.

The Case of Wikipedia

danah: Wikipedia is a really great example of how some of these issues around literacy and knowledge play out. The public's widespread distrust of Wikipedia is deeply disconcerting. Teens regularly tell me that their teachers and parents tell them that it is bad because it can be edited by anyone. The underlying assumption is that experts always produce better content than passionate crowds of amateurs. Studies have shown that Wikipedia is equivalent if not more accurate than Britannica (Giles 2005), but that doesn't satiate critics.

Personally, I see Wikipedia as a phenomenal display of knowledge. Wikipedia articles don't just reveal the final written product. Because of the history pages and the discussion pages, it's possible to see how that knowledge was produced. This allows the viewer to see how debates and disagreements get resolved as editors argue over what is "neutral." My favorite example is the American Revolution article, because both British and American editors had to work together to resolve historical accounts that are often conflicting. Are the people who are fighting revolutionaries or terrorists? What exactly does it mean to be patriotic? Just take a look at the discussion page and you can see how much effort went into trying to resolve conflicting points of view on this one historical item.

Henry: We had a great experience with the New Media Literacies project working with a school in Indiana where Wikipedia was banned from the classroom, not because of anxieties about the quality of information but because some students had been caught intentionally putting up misinformation (Jenkins et al. 2013). We were working on this project around *Moby-Dick*. The teacher really wanted to have the students contribute to the Herman Melville page and had to get permission from the principal. These kids began to enter information they were learning about *Moby-Dick*, and, this being Wikipedia, there were disputes about some of what they put up that forced the students to defend their assertions. In some cases they won, and in some they lost, but at the end they felt an enormous sense of pride at having been able to contribute to the collective production of knowledge. They took away a deeper understanding of the ways knowledge is produced; it doesn't just exist in the pages of a book. Knowledge is under dispute; we don't have a uniform agreement about what the facts are. Wikipedians do agree upon some shared rules to arbitrate disputes, and so the students learned those rules. And, perhaps most importantly, they learned that people have to take personal and collective ownership over the quality of information they contribute to conversations.

Mimi: Wikipedia is a lovely example because information-sharing doesn't just happen. It's highly regulated, organized, and policed. The normative structure of Wikipedia is intense; it's not just a self-organizing hive mind. Just looking at the relationship of an individual to a device or a piece of content doesn't tell you what actually structures reception and influence, which is the social and institutional framework.

We're seeing a blurring between what you would call digital citizenship and media literacy, because those things are becoming much harder to separate. Wikipedia represents a good case to think through these things, because we're all responsible for its quality. It's not a matter of critiquing the experts or critiquing the institutions. If you see something wrong, it's your responsibility to get it fixed. That's the kind of mind-shift that is important from an educational perspective.

Henry: Wikipedia has done a really good job as a community, maybe the best job of any participatory community, of articulating its norms, its values, its ethics. There is a clear model for what ethical participation in Wikipedia looks like – a set of articulated standards by which you measure the quality of any given contribution. What is not there yet is a system for ensuring diversity, for reaching out to groups that are under-represented, and for dealing with the problem of systemic blindness to certain kinds of knowledge and perspectives. I'd love to see other participatory culture communities develop this same level of self-reflection and articulate their standards for what they see as a good contribution or beneficial form of participation. That's one reason why it seems important for students to understand how Wikipedia works, because it represents a rich model for thinking about what kinds of norms support participatory culture.

Mimi: I've been following Minecraft for precisely this reason. What's interesting about Minecraft is how different it is from World of Warcraft (WoW) and other massively multiplayer online role-playing games (MMORPGs), which have centrally controlled servers and content.

Anyone can throw up a server and invite people in on Minecraft. Running a server on the player side raises all kinds of issues of shared governance, the control of content, and community norms. Kids gain first-hand experience of what it means when the server isn't maintained based on collective values, because, if a server is poorly run, there's griefing and low-quality content. That experience is completely different from the corporate governed WoW. Given that Minecraft is now one of the best-selling and most played games of all time, we're seeing these experiences percolate among a rising generation. It builds on the kind of learning that kids get when they are negotiating with one another in playground games or social card games like Pokemon, but brings it to the online world. We're running an online summer camp through Minecraft because we see it as a valuable entry point to issues of online social responsibility that can level up to participation in other online affinity groups, whether to do with other games, fandom, or Wikipedia.

What Contributions Are Valued?

danah: I'm curious as to how you two feel about the importance of contribution. When we talk about participatory culture, active engagement is typically valued over consumption. Usually this means focusing on the production side of things rather than critical consumption. This becomes particularly true when systems are used to measure what it means to be participatory. Clicking a "like" on Facebook is more valued than just reading the update. Adding a review to Yelp is more valued than just using the site to get a sense of what services are available. Comments are more valued on Reddit than voting. All of these metrics are driven by the fact that these services rely heavily on the content that users contribute. But what does it mean always to focus on active participation, regardless of the quality of that contribution? What does it mean to be a part of the system without necessarily giving back? Can someone be a valuable and participatory lurker? What does high-quality listening look like in a networked environment?

Mimi: It's important not to celebrate contribution on its own without considering what kind of collectives we are contributing to. It's about the quality of the contribution but also the broader purpose and agenda. Contribution to a group blog or a peer-governed Minecraft server is different from a Facebook "like" or rating a Netflix movie. Generically, the best way to learn the competencies necessary for thriving in an era of participatory culture involves, in addition to consumption and critique, production, participation, and social connection. I think we need to add to all of this the importance of having that contribution be part of meaningful civic, community, and political engagement. High-functioning affinity groups have ways of elevating and valuing high-quality contributions that are not just about volume or popularity.

Henry: We've been identifying a set of values, things we think are important for young people to understand within a participatory culture, but how do we construct an infrastructure that supports and nurtures these values? We shouldn't fall back on schools and other adult-led institutions as the default mechanism for promoting these skills and norms, since the agendas of schools are not always well aligned with what young people find rewarding about participatory culture. I've written about Harry Potter fan fiction sites as spaces where kids are reading critically, writing, and mentoring each other (Jenkins 2006). But when I talk to educators about the benefits of these practices, invariably someone says that the kids are involved in copyright infringement, they have no respect for other authors, or they're not creative and original. I could celebrate these fan fiction spaces as offering youth a chance to explore and express aspects of sexuality, while someone else would see youth reading and writing pornography. These tensions make bringing participatory cultures into schools especially dicey. The temptation is going to be to police those elements that seem antisocial from the teacher's point of view, to remove those elements that seem controversial with parents, and to protect young people from the consequences of their own decisions. Yet, just as we don't want corporate agents making decisions for us about what constitutes valuable participation, we should be cautious about imposing our own outside perspectives on what makes these sites meaningful to their young participants.

With Harry Potter, we have a group of young people who strongly identify as readers and writers. They are reading a book that centers on a school, Hogwarts; they are identifying with youth, such as Harry and Hermione, who in different ways are exceptional students. These Harry Potter fans would seem to be the kinds of students who would be easiest to connect back to the classroom, to place a positive value on their work. But, even here, we are finding that schools are uncertain about whether or not they can support fan fiction writing as an activity (Stephenson and Belcher 2013). And youth are uncertain about whether it is safe to acknowledge their out-of-school lives in the classroom, given the degree to which they use this forum as a space for exploring transgressive fantasies. After all, those fantasies are at once a normal part of growing up in our culture and precisely the kinds of things from which schools seek to protect young people.

danah: I agree that it's important for us not to impose our ideas of what is *good* participation on young people, but I also think that we need to grapple seriously with the kinds of problematic participation. As I mentioned earlier in this book, there's the case of pro-ana. Pro-ana is both a description of thinspiration content and a term to describe those who view themselves as part of the anorexic lifestyle. Those who subscribe to the pro-ana community see themselves as making a dieting choice and committing to a logic of thinness and restraint. They despise people who pathologize or otherwise medicalize their practices and are deeply resistant to crusaders who are looking to help them.

From a learning perspective, the pro-ana community is pretty amazing. It's quite common for participants to engage critically with the broader media landscape, remix and Photoshop images, and develop new techniques to distribute media content. Some develop technical sensibilities to encode their content so that algorithmic censors by companies who forbid disordered eating content in their terms of service do not delete what they produce. In fact, the notion of "ana" is itself a coded reference. Rather than talking about "anorexia," those in the pro-ana community often refer to their friend "Ana" to minimize the likelihood that they'll be banned. Many pro-anas are extraordinarily technically proficient and deeply thoughtful about media practices. They often refer to their engagement with the anorexic lifestyle as the source of their media and technical literacy. If it weren't for the subject matter that was bringing them together, we would celebrate them. So how do we untangle valuable learning from deeply problematic practices?

Henry: That's a deeply troubling example. Clearly, the learning that goes on there are not the kinds that can or should be embraced by educators. Yet, the challenge is going to be how to create an alternative space that addresses the same kinds of needs that this community serves for its participants. Condemning such values is ultimately not going to be constructive if we are going to help these young people develop a different understanding of their bodies. The more adults push against such practices, the more likely they are to drive young people towards them. Without validating the specific set of beliefs and practices you describe here, we may also need to accept that there are some core needs that youth confront that cannot be addressed by formal institutions dominated by adult values and agendas.

What Interests Are Valued?

Mimi: Only a limited number of interests and identities are validated within schools and peer culture, and either you happen to be one of those kids whose interests are already connected or you're one of those kids who isn't embraced by the school culture, socially, academically, or culturally. There's a strong cultural and institutional bias in many schools that validates interests like football or basketball, specific academic subjects, and extracurriculars such as chess or debate. Even putting aside something as challenging as pro-ana, it's hard for a sci-fi fan or a skater to find a validated place in the school culture.

Katie Salen has written about changing the culture of the school to validate these gamer and geek identities in the Quest to Learn (Q2L) middle school (Salen et al. 2011). Q2L is a public middle school in Manhattan, founded in 2009, which now incorporates grades 6 to 12. Much of the school curriculum includes the input of game designers, and it centers on a game-based pedagogy and problem-solving. What you see in Q2L is a proliferation not just of the empowered geek identity but also kids starting a lot of after-school clubs that are interesting sites of overlap between school, peer, and interest culture. So there'll be a Minecraft club or a video-making club and other interests that aren't fully compatible with the curriculum but are still brought into the schools. This isn't unique to Q2L. Teachers and schools around the country and elsewhere in the world support youth in organizing clubs and in extracurricular and other interest-driven enrichment activities. Given limitations in resources and time, it's often difficult for schools to embrace a really wide range of interests, which is the constant underlying challenge.

Henry: For example, libraries are embracing comics as a way of engaging with young readers and, in some cases, to validate the expertise they already possess, their mastery over domains of knowledge that have not historically been recognized at school. We used to see a student smuggle a comic inside her textbook and have it confiscated by the teacher; now, we see whole library shelves stocked with graphic novels. In our New Media Literacies work, we have an activity where we ask students to map their identities as readers, to identify the many different things they read and write and the roles they play in their lives – from menus and cereal boxes to magazines and websites (Jenkins, Reilly, and Mehta, 2013). We've had any number of students complete the activity and come to the realization that, while schools have long classified them as not very good readers, they read all the time. Reading is a key part of their lives, but they simply don't engage in the kinds of reading that schools value. They don't read the right things or in the right way.

I recall an experience I had in the classroom at the start of my teaching career that still haunts me. I had a student who was performing at a C level and never said anything in class. One day, we started talking about Batman, and he came alive, making many contributions, dominating the discussion. For a solid hour, he got to be the expert and other students were asking him questions. He came to my office afterwards, still aglow, and we talked for another hour or more. This was an incredible, intense moment, where his interests were being valued. Then, two of my literature department colleagues walked down the hall, heard what we were discussing, stuck their head into my office, and said, "What are you doing talking about Batman? This is a literature department!" They were joking with me, but the student's face turned ashen. He stopped talking almost instantly; he wandered away and he said nothing else in the class for the rest of the term.

So, bringing such knowledge into the classroom can be deeply empowering. But this is also an incredibly vulnerable moment, when the slightest negative message will be heard loudly. Schools often give this message – that what matters to young people doesn't matter in school. As they do so, they also signal the opposite – that what matters in school doesn't have any meaning in the rest of your life. We are all about finding those connected learning moments, but we also have to acknowledge how precarious they can be. If students are putting their faith in the system, if they are seeking acknowledgment, and we let them down, that can be devastating. Above all, do no harm.

danah: It's frustrating when youth practices are dismissed by adults because they don't conform to normative understandings of learning. On the flip side, I also meet a lot of young people who have been socialized into a world where any form of adult validation is viewed as negative. Sometimes, this perspective is shaped by broader communities. More often, I run into situations where parents and other family members teach young people not to trust non-family members, including teachers. I recognize how validation by people in power can be quite beneficial for some youth, but I don't think we should take this as a given. It does create new questions and challenges, such as how should we think about diverse mechanisms of validation?

Mimi: While many youth cultures have an oppositional stance to adults, there's generally adult leadership even in the most oppositional ones. I would challenge us to think of any subculture that doesn't have adult heroes and leaders involved in it, which is why adults do have a role to play. I've seen educators who are authentically steeped in the affinity group do this well. It's interesting talking to some of the youth at YOUmedia, a media-production-centered learning lab at the Harold Washington Library in downtown Chicago. The grown-up mentors in interest areas such as spoken word, beat-making, and gaming are not authority figures institutionally in the way that teachers are, but they're people who embody that interest-driven identity, so they have a very different relationship to their kids. Brother Mike, who was the lead mentor for YOUMedia Chicago, is a great example of a poet and a hip-hop artist who had cultural capital with youth. After his tragic death in 2014, Charles Ashby Lewis described him at the memorial service as "a pied piper with dreadlocks." He was known for his signature call and response, where he would say "Power to the people!" and the kids would respond "Right on!" Even teens with a troubled relationship to teachers and education would take advice from Brother Mike about everything ranging from schooling and their writing. Some kids talk about how it's the first time that they were able to be in a space like a library and not be cynical (Larson et al. 2013).

We need translation zones where there's sharing of power between interest-driven, peer-driven, and institution-driven imperatives. The Chicago YOUmedia learning lab, as well as others that are opening up around the country, are examples of experiments in this vein. These are the sites where we see mentors working with young people who have interests such as hip-hop, fashion, or spoken word, and they connect those interests to educational and career opportunity. Taking youth interests and participatory cultures and trying to put them entirely in the classroom is challenging because the institutional imperatives are going to win within the classroom walls. We don't talk about the school as a fully connected learning environment because, most of the time, schools aren't able to focus on this kind of more peer-driven, production-oriented activity that has relevance and visibility beyond the classroom walls. Schools are one important piece of young people's learning ecology, but we have to take the social peer engagement and the diverse interests of kids seriously. Ideally we see schools embracing peer learning and diverse interests within the classroom, as well as connecting to the learning in the wider world. If we can find ways to broker the peace between the cultures of education, entertainment, and youth peer engagement, new media and networked culture can have a huge role to play in expanding these opportunities.

Chapter 5

Commercial Culture

Introduction by danah boyd

As an ethnographer and a geek, I've both participated in and witnessed the development of the current tech ecosystem, the ecosystem usually referred to as "Web 2.0" or "social media" or, increasingly, that which is fueling "big data." I've watched many of those around me ask themselves hard questions about the moral and societal implications of their contributions (boyd and Crawford 2012). I'm in awe of the fundamentally new ways in which people have been able to connect. I'm ecstatic at the possibilities of using data for good; and I still see the internet as my saving grace. But I struggle with my own contributions to both the scene and the industry of technology. When grappling with the uglier side of the industry, I refuse to reject it all or paint complex people in simplistic terms. This means that I get portrayed as an apologist for the tech industry, but this black and white way of thinking about people and their practices is precisely what concerns me when we talk about the commercial nature of the tech industry and participatory culture more generally. If we really want to understand what's unfolding, we need to use different analytic techniques to get a nuanced view of commercial culture. This requires us to move past simplistic explanations and caricatures.

My own love of the internet began when I was a teenager trying to escape the hypocrisy of my hometown. Through the internet, I met people around the world and was exposed to new ideas. This led me to study computer science, originally to do computer graphics. During my collegiate years, I watched the internet go from an esoteric geek space to a venture-backed commercial zoo. I had intended to move to San Francisco and be a part of the tech scene, but, by the time I was nearing graduation, the MBAs had overrun the town, and "big ideas" involved creating new websites that did nothing other than make font sizes bigger for elderly internet users and use their interest in big fonts to provide specialty advertising to the elderly. It was gross, and so I opted for graduate school at MIT. From there I watched the bubble burst in 2000.

I moved to San Francisco in the wake of that explosion, ecstatic to be surrounded by geeks and designers who had happily bid adieu to the financial leeches. By 2003, a new tech scene was buzzing. Product people were gathering with user experience thinkers and coders and tech visionaries. I was the resident scholar, even if my credentials were lacking in an academic sense; I had, after all, just dropped out of graduate school and hadn't re-entered yet. Conferences were held wherever people could get cheap space, and, if the food was free, it was inevitably questionably gelatinous pizza. The signal was loud and clear: it was time to let go of the money and focus on ideas.

There were plenty of people in Silicon Valley in those days who were thinking about creating businesses, folks who thought it was still possible to make it big financially. But they weren't household names yet, "brogrammers" (a derogatory term for programmers for whom machismo is central) weren't a thing, and there wasn't a crazy caste system where status became fraught and contested. Sure, it was hard to ignore certain boisterous people that everyone knew, but the scene was locally defined instead of being shaped by external forces.

The driving frame of the new tech scene was "social software," and the idea was to build new technologies that would allow people to focus on interacting with others. The tools themselves built on a long tradition of practices formally called "groupware," but most of the creators imagined something grander and all-encompassing. Wikis, blogs, social bookmarking, tagging, and social networking were all hot topics.

Many of those in the scene started espousing philosophies that centered on the ways in which technology could transform society for the better. This strain had a long history, especially for those who viewed the internet as a pathway towards societal enlightenment.

As energy built in Silicon Valley, and to a lesser degree in cities like New York and London and Austin, people started paying attention. Conferences hosted by O'Reilly started attracting large audiences, and SXSW-Interactive, a relic of the first wave of internet culture, started exploding. Most of the geeks weren't particularly cognizant of the implications as discussion of Web 2.0 began to unfold (Ellison and boyd 2013). As this term started gaining traction, it quickly became apparent that the concept came to mean different things to different constituencies. From my perspective, there are three core facets: technology, practice, and business.

Among technology-focused geeks, Web 2.0 was a shift in how the web is structured. New tools such as Ruby on Rails, Javascript, and Hadoop opened the doors to new forms of real-time interaction. Syndication procedures and APIs allowed the web to be networked in new ways. The tech focus shifted from the back end to the front end, and the development process went from design–develop–deploy to a culture of the perpetual beta, where constant updates and tweaks made the notion of "shipping" code irrelevant.

As everyday people began embracing the resultant social media tools, a cultural practice emerged that is also called Web 2.0. When people first embraced social technologies during the Web 1.0 era, there was a stark separation between tools used for personal communication – email, instant messenger, etc. – and tools used to create community – MUDs and MOOs, bulletin boards, etc. While interest-based online communities were highly celebrated, most people's mediated communication was private. The new wave of social technologies upended this, blurring interest-based communities and friendship-based interactions and bringing interpersonal activities into the public. Additionally, the rise of the "social graph" (the technology behind the relationships underpinning a social network site) meant that people's conceptions of connection moved away from the notion of group membership to being part of the network. Practically, Web 2.0 ended up meaning social tools designed around the construct of a "friend." This meant understanding the world through social networks – a dynamic which fascinated sociologists and other network scientists, who began obsessing over the new technologies.

As engagement with these new genres took off, business interests kicked in. Venture capitalists, business-minded entrepreneurs, and advertisers wanted to party like it was 1999 again. Those with a passion for monetization flocked to Silicon Valley, and their exuberance and business-speak made "Web 2.0" a buzzword that transcended the original community that was talking about these issues. It's this version of Web 2.0 that began to fragment the scene and propelled the tech industry into the forefront of commercial culture.

Over a decade after it all began, it's hard not to ask critical questions about what's become of the tech industry. At the same time that companies are reaching record high valuations, Silicon Valley is plagued by arrogance, misogyny, and inequity. Following a global economic downturn, politicians everywhere are turning to technology to be an economic savior, oblivious to the costs of giving that much power to a single sector. Market forces are driving questionable trade-offs, prompting the public to use terms like "icky" and "creepy" and "ugly" to describe everything from the pervasive marketing surveillance culture to the economic disruptions that also destabilize everything from employment to social trust.

It is easy to become dystopic, and plenty of early tech evangelists have. Thinkers such as Jaron Lanier and Sherry Turkle – once leading proponents for infusing tech into everything – are now lambasting the industry with equal zealotry. The early Web 1.0 pioneer Ethan Zuckerman (2014) publicly apologized for his contributions to insidious web advertising practices. At the 2014 SXSW conference, in a session hosted by the Electronic Frontier Foundation, two science fiction authors who have been central to the network of geeks surrounding social technologies – Cory Doctorow and Bruce Sterling

– faced off in a debate over whether or not the internet as they knew it was dead or if it could be revived; Cory was far more optimistic and hopeful, but still struggling. Their sentiments reflected the conflicting feelings that many of the geeks in the community are experiencing.

As those inside the tech scene that helped birth the social media ecosystem struggled with their role in it and the wide variation in practices and values, those outside have portrayed Silicon Valley in simplistic capitalist terms. While it's easy to focus on the obscene profits made by tech companies under the umbrella of Web 2.0, it's also important to recognize that economic interests cannot fully explain the norms and culture of Silicon Valley. Many engineers and entrepreneurs have a strong vision about how the world should work, and that often drives their decisions even more than profitability. These values, and the implications of them, are often less visible to critics than the profits made by their companies.

Take, for example, Mark Zuckerberg, the founder of Facebook. Thanks to Facebook's launch on the stock market and the ongoing profitability of the company based on advertising revenue, he's dirty filthy rich. Thanks to his wealth and Aaron Sorkin's depiction of him in the film *The Social Network*, most people believe that money, fame, or girls drive Zuckerberg. Based on my interactions with him, I think that this is an unfair and inaccurate depiction. While we vehemently disagree about how to make the world a better place, Zuckerberg genuinely believes that everyone will benefit if everyday people openly share in public. He sees transparency as the solution to inequality, dishonesty, and intolerance. And he feels that the best way to make this happen is by creating a piece of technology. He also believes that capitalism incentivizes the best minds to work hard, which is why he has structured his business the way he has.

Philosophically, I disagree with Zuckerberg. I think that he's too willing to look the other way as marginalized people are disenfranchised as a byproduct of his efforts to create a more perfect public sphere. And I think that his tools reinforce inequities more than they dissolve them. But I also think that his vision is shaped more by his belief regarding how the world should work than by a capitalist agenda. That said, he now runs a public company and is both beholden to stockholders and the employer of thousands. Vision and beliefs are only one part of people's decision-making logic, but they should not be conflated with capitalism simply because they are embedded inside capitalist infrastructure.

There is no doubt that the logic of capitalism is baked into Web 2.0, but so are various neoliberal and libertarian beliefs. If the tech industry were purely about raw capitalism, the whole goal would be to exploit people for personal wealth. That is certainly happening in some segments of the industry, just as it did in Web 1.0. But part of what makes the tech industry and its widely embraced social tools so complicated is that capitalism cannot fully explain the dynamics here. This creates analytic challenges, because Marxist critiques of social media and the tech ecosystem often miss the mark, failing to get at the nuances that are at play in the development and dissemination of new social technologies. Furthermore, as the tech industry has expanded, non-profit agendas, governmental interventions, and social desires all play a role in shaping participatory culture. These issues are often intertwined in unexpected and under-analyzed ways.

Web 2.0 and Participatory Culture

Henry: Many critical responses to Web 2.0 assume that participatory culture and Web 2.0 are the same thing. They assume that, if they can discredit Web 2.0, they can discredit the concept of participatory culture. One reason why I am increasingly stressing the pre-digital history of participatory culture is to make the point that this struggle to expand the communicative capacity accessible to the public has a much deeper history, that the desire to participate cannot be reduced to the affordances and promises of recent technological platforms.

Web 2.0 initially seemed to embrace the kinds of grassroots communities we've been discussing here, offering some new affordances that have enabled groups to create and share media more easily with each other. But, these companies also sought aggressively to protect the rights of copyright holders, and their very limited grasp of fair use practices constrains the grassroots production of culture. They had to cut deals with advertisers and data-miners and venture capitalists, all designed to make their platforms more profitable. So, whatever the ideals of these technology innovators, underneath the rhetoric of participation are mechanisms of regulation and control. Many of us felt deeply betrayed by the kinds of shifts danah outlines above.

Web 2.0 did represent a fairly fundamental rethinking of how cultural production operates under capitalism, though it did not make producing culture more democratic in any absolute sense. It did broaden who could produce and share culture; it did invite some discourses about responsibility and accountability that have helped to fuel current struggles over corporate terms of service; it did offer a model of cultural and social participation that many found enticing when the terms were first introduced. But those of us who care about the values of participatory culture need to be deeply critical of that move to capture and commodify the public's participatory impulses.

While early explanations of Web 2.0 seemed to imply a simple and transparent congruence between the interests of producers and consumers, every Web 2.0 company, in practice, has faced struggles over the terms of public participation, debates over data-mining and privacy, copyright issues, censorship issues, or concerns over commercialization and branding. Media companies have had to cede some power to their audiences in order to hold onto their loyalty, and, as they do so, networked audiences are increasingly identifying and acting on collective interests. The reality that Web 2.0 platforms over-promise and under-deliver in terms of participation sets the preconditions for these struggles.

danah: As creators and cultural critics, it's easy to be wary of these companies, their agendas, and their promises, but, in watching these shifts unfold, I can't help but hold onto the cultural logic that frames the development of these systems and the various pressures that alter the development of a company and its tools. The creators of most start-ups over-promise, not because they are seeking to deceive, but because they are telling the story of what they *want* to create, the vision that drives their efforts. The question then becomes: what are the forces that prompt a shift in their vision?

The quick and dirty answer is capitalism, but the reality is much more complex. Some people start companies to get rich, but many more start companies with an idea to solve a problem they are experiencing and which they feel is not being addressed adequately by the current set of public and private offerings, whether that problem is finding a date, sharing a video, or finding a house to stay in while on vacation. Founders start piecing together code and, at some point, realize that they need help. They seek money from venture capitalists to keep their venture growing and have to make trade-offs; they hire other people to help them and are forced into learning how to manage people. They have to scale beyond their early adopters and balance the conflicting interests of users. Regulators, journalists, and the public writ large respond to their idea, and they have to find a way to manage everyone's opinion about what should be done. Building these systems to scale is not easy and all sorts of problems come out in the process, highlighting how difficult it is to create something that matters to many people. The story of Web 2.0 began with a vision, but sustaining it required navigating people, capital, and cultural dynamics.

Mimi: What you are both describing with Web 2.0 has a family resemblance to the soul searching that happens when cult media and subcultures go commercial and mainstream. Web 2.0 has become a boundary object between stuff that the subcultural geek values and business, and that's why it feels so contested. It makes sense that the fans and other groups associated with the subcultural side of things have an ambivalent relationship with Web 2.0 because it sits between grassroots and commercial forms of participatory culture.

I want to call attention to two other tech players that define contemporary participatory culture and are at least as important as the Web 2.0 scene: I think of the big three tech industries for participatory culture as Web 2.0, gaming, and mobile. Those three streams came together at a particular historical moment to produce what we think of as today's digital and networked participatory culture. And these three industries also have different relationships to the folks formerly known as the audience and have taken different strategies, with different cultural and subcultural capital associated with them.

Gaming is in some ways positioned as an entertainment subculture, similar to how geeks are a tech subculture. Mobile is another case entirely. It was driven by mainstream kids and consumer-facing mass technologies rather than marginal geeky ones. Mobile was not a communication practice driven by subcultural groups and signaling, and it was from the beginning a space dominated by massive consumer technology players. It has a very different origin story than the internet, which had its high-class idealistic origin story, and gaming, which came from a comparatively lowbrow geek DIY oppositional subculture. Texting culture had a populist origin from the start.

Kids growing up with all three of these technology worlds at their fingertips look to games, mobile, and internet culture for different kinds of social and participatory needs. All three of these industries are adapting in tandem with the growth of participatory culture, changing how they interface with their users, fans, audiences. When I started my research on children's software and games in the 1990s, it was all about shipping shrink-wrapped CD-ROMs to highly defined market niches and throwing the product over the fence to players. Then internet distribution and networked gaming came along, and suddenly the distance between the player and developer narrows dramatically. Players are not only in constant communication with the industry, but they begin actively to mod and hack games in ways that erode the boundaries between players and developers. More recently, mobile has added the dimension of constant and ubiquitous contact. It's been fascinating observing this increasingly intertwined development happening from the vantage point of Los Angeles and the entertainment industry as well. Now, with mobile, net, gaming, and entertainment culture totally intertwined, you're seeing the DIY hacker orientation of gamers playing in the same space as the social connectivity of mobile and peer-to-peer colliding with longstanding popular culture practices. The norms and values driving the industry side are being cross-pollinated too.

danah: Technology development was historically a process of design, develop, and deploy. As I mentioned earlier, Web 2.0 introduced the perpetual beta, which means that nothing was ever completed in design or development before being shared with users. As a result, we see the explicit co-construction of technological systems, as opposed to the social construction of technology that many technology scholars discussed in previous generations (Bijker, Hughes, and Pinch, 1987). Not only are companies not throwing software over the fence any longer; they're also watching users and trying to iterate in response to them. Dan Perkel's (2008) work on "copy-paste literacy" within MySpace is a great case study for highlighting how big companies are reacting to and engaging with users.

Early on, MySpace basically screwed up. They didn't have the technical tools to check all of the things that people fit into the forms they were asked to fill out for their profiles. A young woman figured out that she could put in HTML code, and she started putting in HTML code to modify her profile. Engineers in the company recognized this within twelve hours, but they decided not to respond in order to see what would happen. What emerged was this unbelievable community of people figuring out how to modify their profiles, trade layout and background code, and otherwise alter their MySpace profiles in innovative ways. Some at MySpace wanted to put a stop to this practice, especially since a lot of the mods were particularly hideous – replicating the style of 1990s GeoCities – but MySpace's executives decided that more was to be gained by letting the users maintain control. They only stepped in once this loophole started getting abused by scammers, phishers, and others with more malicious intentions. Over and over again, we see companies building features in response to user practice while users continue to push the boundaries of the technologies' design.

Mimi: What you describe in the MySpace case reminds me of how Japanese mobile providers stumbled on text messaging after they saw teenage girls sending messages through their pagers. Over time, opportunistic response to accidental discovery of user innovation has evolved into a more explicit set of values and practices on the industry side. In addition to getting more effective at capturing and capitalizing on user and player innovation, tech companies try to benefit from the halo associated with a more populist or democratic approach. Even with this adaptation, though, they are often playing a catch-up and appropriation game in relation to user-generated innovation and values. Tech companies are trying to frame these moves in ways that are advantageous to their agenda, but it's not always clear that they are steering the ship. It's tempting to think of people like Jobs or Zuckerberg as overlords with a master plan, but the reality is much more complex. They could also be seen as figureheads for movements that already had momentum.

Core to the success of tech enterprises is not only engineering and innovation, but also active listening and methodologies for capitalizing on trends and creativity cultivated in the wilds of the networked world. The positive spin is that the industry is responsive to user and player needs. The negative spin is that it is exploitative because economic value accrues only to the capitalists. It's important to acknowledge the diversity of players – political and commercial, as well as everyday folk – who are driving change and innovation, whether it is teenage girls in Japan, entrepreneurs in Ghana, or WoW players in China. In an eagerness to critique the tech sector, I see a tendency to over-ascribe agency to Silicon Valley just because there's a handful of geek boys making a lot of money. It's important to keep in mind that Web 2.0 is a parochial concern of a narrow segment of a specific industry sector, albeit an influential one.

Henry: You're insisting on the multiple motives within any given sector, which is realistic. There's a tendency for Web 2.0 critics to strip away all of the details you two are talking about. The cynical perspective is that capitalism always works the same way – nothing really changes. These critics can sustain those claims by flattening out motives. There is a tendency to say that capitalists are only interested in making money, and not to recognize that many of them individually, even many companies collectively, have a social vision that also defines their goals (as, for example, danah's reference to Zuckerberg's social vision).

There are sharp disagreements, debates, and contradictions within companies that are not clear if we simply look at their organizational charts or trace their financial holdings. In many ways, these companies are dysfunctional families, where different units are often competing with each other for resources. Competing visions of the future are pit against each other at every board meeting, with the result that change within the corporation is often one step forward and one step back.

danah: It goes beyond self-justification and conflicted motives. We can critique what Web 2.0 became, but it's also important to understand where it came from. Web 2.0 set itself as different from what gets retrospectively called Web 1.0. But what is Web 1.0? Is it the dot-com boom, defined by e-commerce and vaporware products created by marketers to capitalize on investor interest? Or does Web 1.0 consist of homepages like those on Tripod and "virtual" communities like the WELL that early technology evangelists such as Howard Rheingold and Stewart Brand celebrated? Or is Web 1.0 the technical architecture comprised of HTTP, URLs, and HTML that was at the computational heart of the World Wide Web?

It's easy to find capitalism and greed in Web 1.0 too. In the late 1990s, San Francisco was dripping with MBAs looking to make a buck on inane ideas that they sold to venture capitalists. But that wasn't the whole story. That wasn't the Web that I fell in love with. Still, when the dot-com boom fell to its knees, I was stunned at how many journalists, investors, and Marxist academics pointed to the crash as proof that the whole Web thing was just a fad. They did so because all they saw was the commercial component. I fear that we're replicating that cycle.

Henry: One of the places where Web 2.0 rhetoric distorts our understanding of participatory culture has to do with the ways it represents the collective production of knowledge. O'Reilly's original "What Is Web 2.0" (2005) focuses its discussion of "harnessing collective intelligence" around the blogosphere and also around people adding hyperlinks to existing websites. These are activities that are publicly visible, consciously performed, and involve some degree of collaboration and deliberation. Published just four years later, "Web Squared" (O'Reilly and Battelle 2009), however, is a product of the era of big data and, as a consequence, depicts a considerable loss of collective agency in shaping the directions of the culture. It's about data shed unknowingly by users in the process of conducting their business and social lives online, but not about the conscious efforts of groups of people to reshape the technological environment to better serve their shared interests. This shift more or less reflects changes in the business environment and provides a rationalization for the kinds of data-mining practices that are more and more dominant in corporate America.

Mimi: Participatory and networked culture is forcing us to confront these relationships between individual and collective agency in fascinating ways. People across cultures are being pushed to grapple with concepts like hive mind and network intelligence which see the individual and the collective are inseparable. It's one thing to grapple with these issues in the abstract and another to grapple with them experientially and pragmatically through online sharing, privacy settings, and peer production. This vocabulary of collectivism is even filtering into the US mindset, which has been so committed to seeing individual and collective interests as inherently in conflict.

How Do We Sustain a Participatory Culture in a Commercial Ecosystem?

Mimi: Shifting gears a bit, can we talk about alternative governance and revenue models that reflect the spirit of participatory culture? Is it possible to create sustainable organizations and revenue models that are not completely driven by shareholder interests and traditional business models? Can we maintain, or maybe recover, a sense of the public interest and the public sector in digital and networked culture? Whether it's to do with fandoms, Minecraft servers, or Anonymous, the online world has spawned a whole range of networked collectives that are organized based on a range of community governance models. A cluster of organizations have been building on these models of networked governance – for example, Mozilla, Wikimedia, Electronic Frontier Foundation, Creative Commons, Digital Public Library of America. Some of these models look like traditional non-profit and public-sector models, but some, such as Mozilla, are hybrid commercial and non-commercial models, where they derive commercial revenue to support a non-profit mission, which I think is interesting. Obviously the idea of hybrid economic models has been getting more visibility after Larry Lessig's book *Free Culture* (2004) and with the growth of crowdsourcing, crowdfunding, and the resource-sharing economy. Taking a knee-jerk anti-capitalist stance can stand in the way of thinking creatively about possible alternatives to purely profit-driven and more exploitative modes of capitalist value creation.

In addition to the hybrid model of Mozilla, Wikimedia stands out because there's no advertising on it, and yet it's sustainable. I had assumed that it was sustainable because of grants and fundraising, but it's not. It's completely community-sustained, and it's a demonstration of the fact that there are possibilities for alternative models that get past the polarization of capitalists versus critics.

danah: I would disagree with the idea that Wikipedia is inherently sustainable. It's as sustainable as public media like NPR or PBS. It hosts an annual beg-a-thon, relying on people to sustain it because they're passionate end-users. It's able to do this because wealthy people are passionate about the service and have a commitment to a specific vision of the public good. But each year the beg-a-thon gets lengthier and more invasive. The costs of maintaining Wikipedia grow, but the cachet of the site loses its luster. As a result, I often wonder how long it can self-sustain through this route. More importantly, many other kinds of services can't be sustained through beg-a-thons.

Mimi: The reality of Wikimedia right now *is* that it is self-sustaining and none of us have the crystal ball as to whether it will survive that way in perpetuity. Just like your local NPR station, it is largely privileged folk who provide that revenue. I object to the begging metaphor because it implies that Wikipedia provides no value. I also have no problem with people with more wealth footing the bill for open resources with collective value, and this should be celebrated and recognized. The question is whether this model would work for other organizations and media types.

danah: Don't get me wrong – I am a huge fan of the patronage system, but I also believe that social services should be paid for by taxing the wealthy, and this makes me a heretic in many circles. I also think that Wikipedia is extraordinarily valuable. I just get nervous about claims that a model that relies on annual fundraising and benevolent patrons is inherently sustainable. And I refer to it as a beg-a-thon because the language that the site uses during these fundraising efforts is designed to leverage people's emotions and make them feel obliged to contribute.

Henry: These questions about sustainable alternative models offer a way of moving this conversation forward. We need to have a critical response to the current media environment that reflects both our hopes for the possibilities of collective action within a networked culture and our concerns at the ways that any data we shed can and will be used against us in the marketplace. So many of the academic critics of Web 2.0 stop short of proposing viable alternatives that might allow us to seize some of the opportunities many of us recognized in the early days of the Web. If you start from the premise that everything companies do is by definition evil and corrupt, then you've opted out of participating in the conversation about what ethical, sustainable, community-oriented uses of social networking tools and media-sharing platforms might look like. If you fall back on ideals about the purity of public media, that's probably not going to be what sustains large numbers of experiments in the long run. We need to ask what happens when communities that began by seeing themselves as alternative to dominant social, political, economic, or cultural practices are becoming so dependent on an infrastructure that's driven by commercial motives.

Mimi: Without being too much of a Pollyanna, I wonder if we can ask how grassroots and participatory culture can exploit commercial culture rather than always assume that directionality goes the other way. I watch kids being incredibly resourceful about getting content for free; I watch how industries like record labels and traditional journalism have been seriously challenged and downsized; and I watch how big auto manufacturers are developing products that enable car-sharing. This isn't simply "power to the people!" But there are a broad range of actors who take part in tech innovation, and commercial industries are not the ones controlling major cultural shifts. Acknowledging that people are making money off participatory culture is not the same as saying it's all driven by capitalist incentives and values. I see a real questioning among young people, particularly with the collapse of the labor market for middle-class jobs, about whether capitalism can really deliver on the promise of a better life for the 99 percent.

Fan Culture and Free Labor

Henry: Let me pick up the story from a fan's perspective. Fans were early adopters and lead users of Web 2.0 platforms; they were quick to embrace LiveJournal, Facebook, Twitter, and Second Life. Fans were early in experimenting with podcasting, blogging, and mp3 files. While we could see some reduction of the social vision in the ways Web 2.0 companies described these relationships, there also were many points of overlap between the social vision of these companies and the ways that fans described their shared ideals as a community.

The moment I, and many other fans, woke up to the dangers of Web 2.0 was prompted by a company called FanLib, which decided to take a Web 2.0 approach to fan fiction writing. It started out harmlessly enough – working with rights holders to get them to sponsor official fan fiction contests around minor cult series, just to test the waters to see if fans and companies could work together in this way. But FanLib wanted something more – to become *the* platform for fan fiction on the web. They tried to aggressively undercut some of the platforms that had emerged from fandom itself, recruiting the most visible fan writers and bringing them on board. FanLib adopted a much more corporatized language to speak to the rights holders, suggesting in one prospectus that it was going to teach fans how to "color within the lines." The fans soon saw the company trying to make a profit off fan fiction writing without taking any legal responsibility to defend the community against any legal ramifications and, perhaps, offering them space to publish their work in return for accepting lots of regulation over their content.

This whole proposition contrasts sharply with the fan community's long tradition of seeing stories as gifts shared within a circle of friends. In some cases, the stories are written for specific individuals even though shared more broadly. In all cases, they were labors of love for which no one expected compensation. There had been longstanding and very nuanced debates about what forms of revenue from fan publishing would constitute profiteering. Can you make enough from selling a zine to recoup its production costs? Why should we charge more for a print zine than what it cost to print? Can we charge travel to fan conventions or shipping in order to distribute the zine, given that the fans also want to go to the convention for pleasure, and not all fans can afford to attend? And now, this company was moving into a community that had clear ethics governing economic transactions, trying to turn fan fiction from a gift into a commodity.

One outgrowth of these debates around FanLib was the creation of the Organization for Transformative Works, which was designed to enable the fan community to defend its own traditions and protect its own rights to cultural participation. Fan lawyers agreed to defend fans who faced legal pushback for their creative expression. Fan academics created an online journal that would promote the field of fan studies. Fan programmers and entrepreneurs created alternative social media platforms, such as the Archive of Our Own, which would support the sharing of fan works without having to accept the terms offered by Web 2.0 companies. These developments were occurring at the same time that academics were beginning to express their concerns about Web 2.0, and especially their critiques of the "free labor" behind user-generated content (Terranova 2003) – that is, the rhetoric of web 2.0 presumes a world where companies are able to tap into various kinds of "user-generated content," content that emerges from the creative contribution of participants who, like fans, are motivated to share what they create with others without payment.

danah: It's important to situate labor in participatory culture in light of broader shifts in how labor is constructed. I grew up in a community defined by blue-collar and agricultural labor during the period in which it was shifting to low-status white-collar and service labor. These shifts had serious consequences. Many in my community experienced the shift from factory to service labor as emasculating. Meanwhile, the rise of the so-called creative class was viewed with disdain. I can't tell if this was a product of how education was viewed or if it was simply because it was hard for those in my town to get their head around that kind of labor as work.

In this same vein, there was a lot of creative output that wasn't even seen as labor at all. This didn't mean that people weren't involved in garage bands and hoping that they'd one day be famous. Or that they weren't making quilts for family members that could've been sold. It's just that there was a stark separation between what was constructed as labor and what was understood to be in the realm of family and community, hobby and pleasure.

Fast forward twenty years, and scholars are talking about how people should be compensated for their creative labor. The assumption is that anything that people do that creates capital for someone should be narrated as labor and monetized by all. I can't help but feel really icky about that, not because I don't think people should be compensated for labor but because I think that there's a social cost to understanding every act of production as labor. Once you think of your activities in the frame of labor, the question of worth emerges. How valuable is your production compared to others? And the reality is that we don't treat people's contributions equitably.

I ran into this personally with my blogging. When bloggers were putting advertising on their websites, I was pressured to do so. Some of my friends were making tens of thousands of dollars per month. Yet, I made a conscious decision not to monetize my blog, even though it cost me to sustain it. I realized that I didn't want to understand my blogging in those terms. I didn't want to think about how many people viewed my content or how profitable my audience could be. I literally never looked at my traffic because I didn't want that to be my frame of reference for my production. I didn't want to see blogging as labor. I still don't. And it pains me when people tell me that my blogging for free results is a devaluation of journalists' production of content. But I also fully understand that my ability to make these decisions stems from my privilege of not having to try to find ways to monetize every action I take.

Henry: Critics are concerned by the exploitative nature of such arrangements – the ways that content produced for pleasure is nevertheless sold for profit. Some are worried, as danah suggests, that "free labor" will squeeze out paid labor for creative workers. Others are concerned by the core inequalities of who does and who doesn't get paid for what they create. The term "free labor" implies that what's exploitative about this is that people are not being paid, while companies are making money. But, much like danah and her blog, many participating in these practices do not want to see what they've created become commoditized; the act of paying them would pull them deeper into the commercial system, whereas what they want is to remain largely outside it.

So, should people get paid for contributing content to YouTube? Some YouTube content is professional or semi-professional in origin, and there is a strong desire for payment to minimally sustain future production. Independent media-makers are seeking support for their work and need to be paid. Film students are producing "calling card" movies in the hope of being hired to work within the media industries.

There would ideally be some system whereby these people could recoup the costs of their production or perhaps earn a living based on what they create. But if you are using the platform as a personal archive to share home movies with your loved ones? Maybe not. The idea of "selling" that content is morally disgusting.

In some odd ways, the critical studies discourse about "free labor" as exploitation is simply the flip side of the industry claiming that, if we create a more open-ended system of copyright and fair use, people won't produce if they can't get paid for their work. They see creative expression as purely an economic activity, without understanding the underlying social and cultural reasons why people in a participatory culture might create and share media with each other. At the same time, we need to be concerned about who has the time and resources to participate in these kinds of informal, unpaid cultural exchanges. Does participation without concern for compensation represent a form of middle-class privilege? Does it continue a long tradition where women have been encouraged to contribute their creative work as a form of charity, while men have consistently sought to professionalize creative labor as part of their livelihood?

Mimi: Much of the debate fails to recognize how most cultural and knowledge production has been more social than commercial in nature. Most labor and contributions we make to society are unpaid. When we talk about labor in a capitalist society we're talking about a very narrow band of contributions to society. The fact that these exchanges are happening on commercial platforms is what is different today, not the fact that these contributions are noncommercial in nature. One under-appreciated aspect of the growth in online labor is that the ethic of free contribution was driven forward by students, who comprised a significant proportion of the early internet population. Students in residential colleges and universities are a highly literate population who are not yet participating fully in the labor market and have the time and resources to contribute to free culture. In my research with fan subtitlers who were competing with commercial localization firms (Ito 2012b), the bulk of them were college and high-school students, and they "retired" from these kinds of activities after finishing school and entering the formal labor market. As the internet has gone more mainstream, this population is being pushed further into minority status, which may be one of the reasons why you see the free labor issue becoming more contentious.

Given this broadening demographic of net participation, it is healthy to start monetizing some of what was historically non-monetized. That's what's interesting about the so-called sharing economy, crowd-funding, and crowdsourced labor like Airbnb, Kickstarter, car-sharing, or time-banking. People are experimenting with new ways of raising money and exchanging goods and labor that used to happen informally, without the mediation of massive markets. The ideology that it is corrupting to monetize "labors of love" was a side effect or a resistance to the commodification of labor. We need models that can get past this polarization. Juliet Schor has been leading research on these new kinds of resource-sharing marketplaces and the emerging values surrounding them, which are often centered around community-building and alternative lifestyles (Carfagna et al. 2014; Schor and Thompson 2014). There's a curious mix between people who use these kinds of barter and sharing systems out of economic necessity and those who see them more as a lifestyle choice.

It's an open question whether crowdsourced and P2P marketplaces will be the latest step in dehumanizing and instrumentalizing labor. Hopefully these new markets will promote more ecological and values-driven ways of sharing goods and labor in ways that help people build relationships and communities. The devil is in the details of how these markets are organized. Some, like traditional time banks and food swaps, are tied to a set of strong community norms that build social capital. The challenge here is that these networks can be exclusionary to people who don't share the same culture and values (DuBois, Schor, and Carfagna 2014). On the other hand, a platform such as UberX or TaskRabbit has lower barriers to participation, but it isn't animated by the same spirit of shared culture and community that you see with the more hipster-inflected kinds of peer markets. We're seeing a complex alchemy of people participating in more transactional versus more community and values-driven ways.

Henry: There have historically been two different ways fans related to the idea of cultural production as paid labor, both heavily coded in gender terms. Since the 1920s, almost every major science fiction writer, editor, agent, and illustrator started as a participant in the science fiction fan community. Fandom became a support system that allowed them to acquire their skills and move into the professional sphere. There was a robust system for recruiting new professionals. This is the way the system worked for many men.

For most of that period, women were totally or largely locked out of that system of professional mobility. Some did make it through this mutual support network. But women often faced a reality that they were not going to be able to go from writing *Star Trek* fan stories into producing, directing, or writing *Star Trek* episodes. Instead, for many reasons, they embraced a discourse that condemned fans who profit off other fans. This is what I mean when I describe fandom as a contemporary form of gift economy: fandom still exists in relation to commercial culture; it is never fully autonomous, insofar as it builds on shared responses to commercially produced work, but there's a strong value placed on creating and exchanging culture among community members to enhance the collective good and not for personal gain. There was a strong feminist politics undergirding these shared ethical norms. But critics like Abigail De Kosnik (2013) argue that this prohibition also resulted in the failure to construct an infrastructure that led from amateur creativity to professional opportunities for women.

The publication of *Fifty Shades of Grey* may represent a substantive shift in these different regimes of value. This mass-market best-seller was revised from what had originally been the author's *Twilight* fan fiction. E. L. James has been open about her origins in fandom in a way that many other women (Cassandra Claire, for example) who "went pro" sought to mask their roots, or to remove their fan fiction from the web, on the advice of their agents and publishers. For women, professionalization meant breaking with fandom, whereas men enjoyed scaffolding as they made this transition. Now that the media has picked up on the fan fiction origins *of Fifty Shades*, they are seeking out other fan writers. Will this burst of publicity be enough to change things? It's too early to tell, though Amazon's summer 2013 announcement of Content Worlds, a program which would allow fan fiction writers to sell their stories for profit online, can be seen as an indicator of things to come, one which has been met with profoundly mixed feelings within fan circles.

Some are arguing that the forms of social exchange within fandom – where people build freely on each other's works, developing often shared interpretations of who these characters are, giving each other feedback on stories, and otherwise collaborating in the development of new material – depend heavily on the idea that no one can profit from these shared activities. The news media have focused some on the intellectual property issues: if *Fifty Shades* is heavily derivative from *Twilight*, then what does E. L. James owe to Stephanie Meyer (2008) for creating the intellectual property on which this novel was built? But these questions do not respect and reflect upon the communal mode of production, the shared creative energies on the fan side, which went into shaping this now commercialized narrative.

danah: In our society, labor is often constructed as individual work. But even creative labor that is imagined to be about the individual is almost always the product of deep collaborations and extensive support. Consider how a supposedly single-author book is made. The author's ideas are shaped by the people with whom she interacts. While she might write the text, it's inevitably reviewed by other people, edited by other people, formatted by other people, etc. Some of the people get credit in the form of acknowledgments, but most are recognized only under the umbrella of the publisher. Then, when the book goes from words to print, all sorts of other people are involved in getting the book in your hands: publicists, printers, deal-makers, book-sellers, postal workers, etc. This is all invisible to those who are consuming the book. The focus is on the author because the creative labor is always what matters most. I don't see a lot of thinking about how labor operates within networks and how those networks need to be recognized and supported – and not just financially.

Mimi: In addition to fandom, the gaming industry has put forward different models of collective and "derivative" kinds of cultural production. Just as fan production has been considered "derivative," modding used to be considered marginal and unauthorized. In the most recent generation of many PC games, though, the industry has moved to a stance of full-on embrace and actively develops assets and supports for modding communities. We even see pathways to monetization being supported by the industry in some cases.

Fandom has been playing with these boundaries for longer. In the Japanese fan comics scene, you very rarely get an individual author because of the intensive labor of drawing comics. Comics are drawn by groups known as "circles" and are sold predominantly in P2P markets where fans sell to other fans. In Japan these P2P markets are massive in scale and take over the largest convention centers in the country. The fan industry isn't at the scale of professional circulation in terms of the quantity of revenue generated, but it is still massive. In the largest market, which runs twice a year in Tokyo, 600,000 people show up to buy and sell amateur comics. Many versions of this event run all over the country. This is a historically well-established, revenue-generating, completely P2P network of markets for derivative work. Many people have sustainable lifestyles based on creating and distributing their own work, and some of them convert to a traditional commodity market by publishing commercially. But many artists just stay completely within the peer-to-peer marketplace (Tamagawa 2012).

The fan comics scene in Japan is just one historical model where production is decoupled from a contractual labor relationship or a commodified media market. The online world has obviously made these P2P markets for both labor and goods much more accessible and more visible. We're clearly still in the early years in the development of these new models of scaling informal and P2P markets, and we don't know yet what kind of a challenge they will pose to existing corporate actors in most sectors.

Inside the Belly of the Beast

Henry: danah, so far in the conversation, of the three of us, you often have been the most critical of corporate actors, yet you have worked for numerous companies – Intel, Google, Yahoo!, and now Microsoft. How do you reconcile your ideological commitments with your professional life?

danah: As an idealistic but naïve teenager, I had some pretty entertaining but simplistic beliefs about different sectors. Over the years, those were quickly shattered. I believed that those in government must be brilliant because they had so much power. When I started spending time with elected officials, I was horrified to learn the darker sides of power. In college, I became a passionate activist, and I foolishly believed that those who went to work for the greater good of humanity must be saints. I was devastated to learn otherwise, particularly when I watched a group of activists try to challenge the status quo by developing a different status quo. In academic contexts, I was disappointed to find professors who believed themselves to be divorced from the oppressive systems that they critiqued while sitting in elite institutions that cost more per year than my mother made and owned more property than the Astor family.

Given my activist roots, I was prepared to hate corporations. I hadn't put corporations – unlike government agencies, non-profits, and educational institutions – on a pedestal. And, as a result, I was actually surprised to learn that many people within corporations were very critical of the institutions they were a part of, very passionate about making institutional change, and very determined to leverage the beast they were a part of to do the right thing.

I was also surprised by just how honest companies were – about their protocols, their incentives, their limitations. To my surprise, I felt as if the fights that I had at companies were more ethical than anything I ever had in academia or with non-profits. I could point to specific protocols, highlight the unfairness or problematic nature of decisions, provide data that challenges the assumptions . . . and people would listen!

When I was working in non-profits, I felt as if everything always boiled down to a loyalty question. In other words, how dare I challenge a particular decision, because we were all in this together to make the world better. Nothing made me angrier than non-profits that refused to pay employees a livable wage, for example.

There's a lot that I don't like or trust about corporations, but I've come to respect their strengths and limitations. And I'm regularly surprised by how many corporate employees genuinely want to do the right thing. I think it's easy for academics to hate corporations and reject corporate influence on participatory culture. Philosophically, I have major problems with capitalism, but I also accept that we live in a capitalist society. I don't think it's productive to automatically dismiss anything that is a product of capitalism just because I don't like our economic model. But, as a result, whenever I defend a practice or product that comes from a corporation, I'm dismissed as a sell-out.

Because the three of us have not been viciously anti-corporate, we've often been attacked for being too friendly to commercial interests. I'm disturbed and disappointed by scholars who are unable to see nuance in their critique of capitalism and those who engage with it. Having worked inside and around corporations for the better part of a decade, I've come to accept that corporate interests are a part of the ecosystem and that it's healthier to engage them than to pretend that they don't exist. Yes, there are serious power issues at play, but it's complicated.

Henry: What roles do you think companies could legitimately play in dealing with inequalities and access and participation?

danah: This is tricky. And it depends on what kinds of companies we're talking about. Usually, when this notion is put forward, there is an expectation that big for-profit companies should have a societal responsibility. But, in the United States, public for-profit companies have a legal fiduciary responsibility to their shareholders. Very few companies are structured around what's called a "double bottom line," or a measure of the social impact of the company. As a result, these companies can actually be liable to their shareholders if they do things that go against their bottom line. Even the notion of "corporate social responsibility" is often narrated through a marketing framework. With smaller companies like startups, the issue is often more about capacity. They're just trying to figure out how to survive.

Interestingly, underneath the corporate agenda are a whole slew of individuals who often want to give back. Sometimes, they do this through personal "off-hours" work, but I often find employees who get creative in aligning social missions with their corporate goals. This is where you see true innovation emerge. And alignment of missions and mandates is one of the most successful ways of making sure that a company does the right thing. Take something like diversity, a value that many progressives have. Most of the people that I know who have pushed diversity goals within companies do so by making visible the data that show that their company performs better when they have diverse employees.

Don't get me wrong – I think we need to critique the very foundations upon which corporations are built. American capitalism is structured predominantly around maximizing profit by any means. The changes that I think are necessary to address the inequities we're talking about require fundamentally calling capitalism into question. I don't see a way in which the inequities are cleanly resolvable otherwise. But I'm still excited by the innovation that comes from the constraints of a company when really good people have to work within systems or around limitations in order to do something that they feel is meaningful.

The Place of Policy

Henry: When I think of the work that I do in engaging with industry, I think about it as policy intervention. In the UK, Canada, Australia, and New Zealand, there's a long tradition of cultural and media studies people who are involved in policy discussion, trying to shape the cultural agendas of their government. They often make a set of choices to work with governments they disagree with. They're not going to get everything they want, but participating in the process and putting pressure on those systems to enable things they care about is part of what it means to be a cultural scholar in those countries. In the United States, cultural policy, for the most part, is not set by government – educational policy may be an important exception here. But US cultural policy, I would argue, is set by corporations. Where digital media are concerned, policy often ends up being part of the terms of service. To change that, you actually have to engage the companies. You can't "speak truth to power" if you're not speaking with those in power.

I never feel more political than when I'm standing in a corporate boardroom challenging assumptions about how a company treats fans and how their core policies affect young people's lives. I don't start from a premise that these people are evil capitalists who have no souls. I start from the premise that they're trying to do the best they can as human beings, within an institutional context that makes it difficult for them to act in certain ways. But, the more I can convince them that they can reconcile their social agendas with what the institutional imperatives are, it becomes more possible for them to act in ways that are accountable and responsible. Having critics come in and speak their language may empower some voices within the company to make a difference in discussions that are taking place in that boardroom, with or without our presence. It gives the progressives in the boardroom moral support; it enhances the credibility of corporate players who are struggling to try and make a difference in these policies. My work with companies has never been about ensuring better, more efficient ways of making money. I'm working with companies because they have an enormous effect on our culture. And walking away from working with companies doesn't allow you to make a difference.

Mimi: I also feel that our public culture is being defined more and more by policies set by commercial actors, and we have to engage. We haven't talked much about policy and government. There's a degree to which participatory culture can be grassroots and emerging, but there are also certain things that really require shared values and collective will. You want a combination of bottom-up norm-setting and smart policy direction. We're completely lacking in the political will for that top-down conversation. danah, that's where your efforts at mitigating some of the most misguided kinds of policy in the online space have been incredibly helpful. In education I feel as if there's very little positive vision for participatory and internet culture in the way that Wikipedia has set generative policies for content contribution. In many ways Google has done more to provide networked learning tools to kids than our formal educational institutions have, but these offerings have not been guided by the kinds of values for learning and equity that we would hope for.

danah: My view on legal regulation is that it's one force for change, but not the only force. I subscribe to the model Larry Lessig (2006) outlined in *Code*, where he argued that all social systems are regulated by four forces: market, law, architecture, and social norms. When those four forces are aligned, change can be quite powerful, but when they are in disarray or at odds, problems often emerge.

Policy in the tech arena is messy. All too often, new policies are introduced for political interests, and those who are making the decisions do not have an understanding of the ramifications of what they're putting forward. Laws are often introduced before technical systems have stabilized and before the public has really engaged with the issues at play. As a result, we see all sorts of unintended consequences, and many regulatory moves intended to protect vulnerable populations backfire. I am often wary of policy prescriptions, not because I don't believe that there's a place for public policy, but because I believe that the policy should be grounded, evaluated, and iterated to keep it true to the intended goals.

Many people know that I'm deeply critical of the Children's Online Privacy Protection Act (COPPA). A decade in, COPPA is used primarily to keep young people off major social media sites under the banner of child safety. Although few companies understand how it functions, it's become a significant disincentive for companies to develop tools for the under-thirteen crowd. When it was first proposed, it was intended to empower parents, but many parents are teaching their children to lie about their age to circumvent age-based restrictions designed by companies whose lawyers tell them to avoid under-thirteens at all costs. This is a law where no one has won except fear-mongers.

I actually believe in the primary goals of COPPA: protect privacy, empower users, etc. But, far from actually protecting privacy, I think that legislation like COPPA creates perverse disincentives that undermine our ability actually to think through what privacy regulation should look like. All too often "protect the kids" is the rallying cry, obfuscating the much harder and more complex issues at stake. What saddens me more is that we have no easy mechanism for evaluating what does and what doesn't work. Laws get entrenched, and it's hard to undo something, even when it's backfiring.

In the realm of participatory culture, we have all sorts of regulatory barriers to innovation that are meant to protect corporate interests or protect people from corporate interests. For example, I'm sure both of you can speak at length about the issues around copyright and remix. One of the challenges of the conversation around privatization and participatory culture is that it often twists the conversation to being about the market versus the law. Technologists often rally to make visible the power of technology, but my interests definitely lie in understanding how social norms shape these systems and how law, tech, and the market are also used to undermine social norms.

Henry: We might make some productive distinctions between privatization at the level of infrastructure, content, and relationships. Each layer represents a significant set of struggles between the historic practices associated with various forms of participatory culture and corporatization.

So, starting with privatization of infrastructure, who owns the space where the key conversations defining the culture get held? If our political life is moving more and more into the digital environment as currently constructed, it's like moving the civic functions of the town square into a shopping mall. Commercial owners do not necessarily allow for collective say in governance, provide insurance of free expression, or actively encourage minority expression that might go against their business interests.

Privatization of content refers to the movement from a folk culture model, where the core stories that we use to make sense of our lives belong to the folk and can be added to freely, towards one where we are increasingly remixing content that originated in commercial culture and where copyright regimes constrain what we can do with these stories.

The issue of privatization of relationships is most visible when we look at social networking platforms. I bring my friends together through Facebook, and what we do there is a byproduct of our social interactions with each other. Yet, Facebook asserts control over that content and makes it difficult for me to export my data and move those social interactions to another networking site. When I sign the Facebook terms of service, I cede control over the most important relationships in my life to a corporate interest; I now have to tolerate all kinds of policies the company may impose at will without consultation with the participants, because it becomes so difficult to start over someplace else.

So, as we think about media policy, we have to factor in each of these forms of privatization and the potential damage it does to our individual and collective rights to participate.

danah: When we talk about participatory culture vis-à-vis regulation and companies, we inevitably talk about the entanglement of people with each other, and yet the American regulatory regime is wholly focused on the individual. While class action suits aggregate people, individual harm and individual rights are still the dominant standards. Many of our legal constructs are not prepared to deal with a networked society. What can and should networked rights look like? Who has the right to my relationships on Facebook? Me? The other people? Facebook? The global nature of this only makes it more difficult to untangle the boundaries, both culturally and with respect to jurisdiction. Whose rights to a particular piece of content matter? What happens when content flows across boundaries? The policy issues around participatory culture are going to get more complicated, not less.

Mimi: The idea of public policy is becoming so hybrid because transnational companies like Facebook are setting policy and regulating behavior, without direct government oversight in most cases. Clearly there are points at which government policy starts impinging on what they do, but historically the governance of public infrastructures doesn't apply to these commercialized network public spaces. That's where we really need a new conversation in the US context.

The US is unique in having this whole layer of non-profit and philanthropic resources tied in complicated ways to political activism. Working with the MacArthur Foundation has been fascinating because its private philanthropy is values-driven but non-governmental. In the best instances it can help mediate grassroots and more elite and institutionalized forms of power. It's fantastic what private philanthropy does in the US. It gives me hope in private individuals and organizations who invest time and resources for social good. At the same time, the burdens on this sector are too great given the needs, particularly in areas like education. Philanthropy can play an important role in providing resources, building networks, and brokering coalitions, but we absolutely have to have robust partnerships across non-profit, commercial, and government sectors to be effective in making any systemic reforms take hold. At the end of the day, I need to be hopeful that these partnerships and coalitions can further progressive agendas. I'd like to stay mindful of the risks but continue to build these connections and positive alternatives.

danah: It's easy to dismiss commercial culture and the technologies that emerge from it because of the capitalist context in which they are embedded, but any analysis of participatory culture needs to stem from what is rather than what should be. Today's technologies are shaped by and help shape the commercial landscape. As a result, much of what we're seeing in participatory culture is affected, for better and for worse, by capitalism and the economic, political, and legal landscape that underpins contemporary business.

Chapter 6

Democracy, Civic Engagement, and Activism

Introduction by Henry Jenkins

My most recent work seeks to understand how the kinds of robust participatory cultures we've been discussing might lead to democratic participation. Given what we've already said about the types of informal learning communities that have emerged in and around digital media, we should not be surprised that these communities play an active role in activities that are preconditions of political engagement. Participatory communities work together to inform each other about the world and teach communication and organization skills. They help each other find their personal and collective voice and provide a context through which they can articulate their common interests and shared values. Ultimately, these communities encourage conversations about social and political change. Often, it takes conscious planning or a dramatic catalyst to transform these latent capacities into direct political action, so researchers working on youth and participatory politics are trying to better understand under what conditions young people begin to think of themselves as political agents.

Beyond the specific mechanisms of participation fostered by such informal learning communities, my current research focus is on what we call "the civic imagination." I use this term to describe the relationship between acts of the imagination and the origins of political consciousness. Before we can change the world, we need to be able to imagine what another, better world might look like. We need to understand ourselves as political and civic agents and as members of particular communities, we need to be able to see making change as possible, and, in many cases, we need to be able to feel empathy for the experience of others.

These ideas have been asserted in different ways across history. Our founding fathers wrote their manifestos under pen names drawn from Greek heroes and Roman orators and cosplayed as "savages" as they dumped tea in Boston Harbor. The civil rights movement of the 1950s and 1960s relied heavily on religious metaphors – "the River Jordan," "the Promised Land" – drawn from the black church tradition. Initially, these metaphors could seem strange to those outside of such movements. For example, the major television networks did not air Martin Luther King's "I have a dream" speech during their coverage of the march on Washington because they saw it as a religious rather than a political message (Bodroghkozy 2012). Today's young people are expressing their political visions, often in a language taken directly from popular culture and through mechanisms and practices inspired by participatory culture.

My own discovery of *Star Trek* in the 1960s and my entry into fandom a few years later was a politically transformative encounter. I was living in Atlanta at the peak of the civil rights era. I lived in a seg-regated neighborhood, went to all-white schools, and the only people of color I encountered were either maids or workers for my father's construction company. Yet, on television, I was seeing a multicultural, even multi-planetary crew work side by side, as friends. They went out to explore the universe together. The program articulated a philosophy that celebrated diversity. And, yes, *Star Trek* often failed to live up to its own ideals, but even its failures created a context where fans could debate what it would mean to live in a more diverse society. When I was old enough to go to fan conventions, I discovered a community of people who were trying to explore what these kinds of open-minded values might mean in the context of their everyday lives. And, along the way, the members of the *Enterprise* crew were joined in my imagi-nation by many other representations of alternative communities who sought to take collective action to make their worlds better places

– Robin Hood's Merry Men, the Knights of the Round Table, Captain Nemo's crew, the Rebel Alliance, or the misfits who venture down the yellow brick road. For me, these stories were the resources through which I forged my political identity and articulated my ideals for what a better society might look like.

Several decades later, one of my graduate-school mentors, John Fiske (1989), wrote about the trajectory of a teenage girl's relationship to Madonna. Fiske was describing what we would now call "identity play." He talked about the value of young people asserting their own voices in public, finding solidarity with other Madonna fans, and articulating a shared sense of female empowerment in their society. Fiske hinted that one's engagement with popular culture might inspire shifts in one's political identity. He was encountering some early signs of what would be called "third-wave feminism," which was strongly connected both to the process of finding one's voice through DIY media and with feminist politics expressed through popular culture (especially music and comics). His Madonna fans would soon become Riot Grrrls. The Riot Grrrls were young feminists, associated broadly with the punk movement, who rejected feminine stereotypes and asserted their rights to full participation, often via their production of zines, comics, and a range of other DIY media practices. But the loose sense of "resistance" in 1980s cultural theory remained disconnected from more rigorous definitions of what constitutes the political. Fiske did not engage with the concerns of political scientists, who understood politics primarily in terms of institutional practices, such as voting, lobbying, or petitioning. He was focusing more on the feminist conception that "the personal is political" and saw politics in terms of these young women asserting greater autonomy in their everyday lives through what he called "micro-politics."

As someone who had an undergraduate background in political science, I struggled for some time to reconcile these two conceptions of the political. My research had shown me the ways that participatory culture was enabling people to question and work through their lived experiences of gender, sexuality, class, race, and generation at the micro-level Fiske was describing. Through my involvement within fandom, I was also seeing people apply skills they had acquired through their recreational lives to activities that would be defined as political by even the most traditional definitions. I was watching fans become activists and even seeing the emergence of organizations that explicitly supported such a transition. For example, many fans confronted struggles over copyright and fair use. They founded the Organization for Transformative Works, which lobbied on behalf of fans, speaking at governmental hearings to advocate for exceptions to current copyright laws to allow for fan remix practices. My first scholarly works dealt with fandom as a site of grassroots cultural production, a theme that has surfaced multiple times across our discussions, but I could not help notice, especially given my own experiences around *Star Trek*, that fandom was also a space where people were both implicitly and explicitly working through issues of diversity, equality, and social justice.

When the MacArthur Foundation was creating its new Youth and Participatory Politics Research Network (YPP), I really wanted to document and analyze how innovative groups, organizations, and networks were forging more powerful links between participatory culture and civic/political participation. The network has political scientists, philosophers, educators, anthropologists, and youth radio producers, and we've been hearing from scholars from a range of disciplines who are thinking about the political lives of American young people. We've found forms of political participation that are embedded in the everyday life practices of young political agents. In a white paper for the YPP network, Cathy J. Cohen and Joseph Kahne define participatory politics as "interactive, peer-based acts through which individuals and groups seek to exert both voice and influence on issues of public concern" (2012: vi). This report identified various forms of participatory politics, including:

- sharing of information through social media;
- engaging in online conversations through digital forums, blogs, and podcasts;

- creating original content in the form of online videos or Photoshopped memes to comment on a current issue;
- using Twitter and other microblogging tools to rally a community towards collective action;
- building databases in order to investigate an ongoing concern.

It's been great to be part of a multidisciplinary community. I am taking these insights back to my USC team, Media, Activism, and Participatory Politics (MAPP), where graduate students are trying to better understand the routes young people take towards greater civic engagement and political participation. Most of the standard research suggests young people become invested in politics as a consequence of the role models provided by their parents (their political involvement, dinner table conversations), their teachers (especially in civic classes which deal with controversial issues, hear from local officials, or take field trips to see the government at work), and their school communities (extra-curricular activities, community service). But the YPP network is discovering that young people may also be drawn into political exchanges through their informal learning communities, including those around fandom or gaming.

Part of what has made this work possible has been the ways in which the term "participation" forms a bridge between work in studies on participatory culture and work in political theory and philosophy on participatory politics. What we are calling participatory politics refers to the ways that the mechanisms of cultural participation get harnessed for political purposes. For instance, young people who learn how to use a camera recording skateboard stunts end up producing records of protests. Fans creating videos may use remix for other political videos, and those who are writing fan fiction may use those skills to construct arguments designed to mobilize other fans towards civic and political action.

My MAPP research team has moved well beyond a focus on fan activism and towards an attempt to understand many different kinds of change movements, including Occupy Wall Street, Invisible Children

(IC) and *Kony 2012*, the DREAM activists, young Libertarians, and American Muslim youth. Each of these different kinds of community have used new media platforms and participatory culture practices to recruit, train, and support young activists (Kligler-Vilenchik and Shresthova 2012). We've moved from a focus on organizations like the Harry Potter Alliance (Jenkins 2012) to larger networks, which bridge between various groups and individuals and help to coordinate their activities. We now have a much more dispersed and decentralized notion of what activism looks like in a networked culture, though we remain very interested in the trajectories leading participants towards a deeper engagement with political issues.

We see some similarities in terms of what motivates and mobilizes such efforts. The kids that are most political often have a strong artistic side. They are learning to make and share media. And even those groups that seem to embody fairly traditional kinds of identity politics – the DREAM activists, American Muslims – are using reference points from popular culture to describe their political identities and goals. It is not simply that fan activism is a new model for social change, but that the appropriation and remixing of media content has become a tactic widely deployed across youth-oriented political movements of all kinds.

As we look at these spaces, we see a new kind of rhetoric that feels comfortable for this generation of activists, a rhetoric designed to spark the civic imaginations of their participants. Youth have often felt excluded by the kinds of "policy wonk" or "inside the beltway" language used by more traditional organizations. Such efforts assume supporters are already deeply invested in the current political process and know how the system works. They frame politics in terms of specialized knowledge, a sphere removed from the practices of everyday life. The new styles of participatory politics tap into what young people already know as fans, consumers, and participants within social networks and deploy this popular cultural capital as the starting point for political action. We hope this new model may help people who have felt excluded from politics find their way into fuller participation. And so we go back to my core idea that democracy and diversity are at stake when we talk about the value of participatory culture.

Networked Power and the DREAMer Movement

Mimi: We're at a moment when our existing organizations, whether they're political, educational, or economic, are being challenged on a lot of fronts. The move Henry describes from formal institutionalized politics to culturally driven and micro-politics parallels the shift that we're trying to push from education to learning. What does learning and participation look like in collectives where people are not delegating all the authority to organizations in the way that they used to do? I'm not saying this is happening everywhere for everyone, but it is becoming more possible. The cases that Henry is describing are examples of participatory politics enabled by networked collectives and new media. On the learning side, in the Connected Learning Research Network, also part of MacArthur's Digital Media and Learning initiative, we are developing a parallel set of case studies of the democratization of learning in interest-driven online groups.

The problem, of course, is that most people aren't actually engaged in these kinds of groups, even though the internet makes them more accessible. There's incredible potential to increase personal agency in politics and social change. But it's also a scary time, because we're in such big trouble if people can't take responsibility and ownership of their collective participation. We can't stay in the mindset of delegating authority to big corporations and governments. Today we're in an era when many elite organizations don't have the power to regulate in the ways they used to do, and nor do they have the political will to contribute to the public good in the same ways that they have historically. We've seen a gradual erosion of both public and private support for things like social welfare, research, and education and a growing onus on private and personal responsibility. Something like Kickstarter seems very much a sign of our times, for better and for worse. We really need everyday folk to step up and take on responsibilities in public life, whether it is by blogging, organizing, or funding. It's so important that youth develop the capacity for engaging in these ways.

danah: As an activist, I get very excited when youth recognize that they can build meaningful networks and challenge the status quo. Given their limited access to physical public spaces, they often organize through networked publics, using technology to coordinate, communicate, and activate. Of course, their participation in networked publics is simultaneously a source of anxiety for those who are concerned with maintaining the status quo. And, not surprisingly, parents and authorities often clamp down on youth organizing.

I saw this happen in Los Angeles in March 2006. In the previous year, Congress had introduced a Bill – HR 4437, the "Border Protection, Anti-Terrorism and Illegal Immigration Control Act of 2005" – that would treat undocumented people as less than human. Immigration reform activists rallied outraged individuals to protest the Bill, primarily through Spanish-speaking radio and print media. Many youth felt as though their voices weren't being heard, in part because many of them were citizens even if their parents were not. Frustrated, teens turned to MySpace, instant messaging, and cell phones to start organizing their own protest, which was designed to be a school walkout on the Monday following the adult-organized protest. When thousands of teens walked out, they were chastised. Mayor Villaraigosa publicly admonished these teens for being an embarrassment to Cesar Chavez, highlighting how the well-respected activist was a champion for education while these youths were throwing away theirs. Not surprisingly, some of the students who walked out were simply interested in an excuse to skip school. Thus, when the media covered this story, they used truancy and youth safety as their frames. What the media didn't address was how the state of California fined the city of Los Angeles for each absent student. Furthermore, no one stopped to pay attention to how, after years of complaining about teens' failure to engage in political issues, these teens did something pretty phenomenal and classically political, only to be dismissed and ignored.

Henry: But the story doesn't end there. DREAM activism moved beyond that initial disappointment. While the established immigrant rights movement was pushing for comprehensive reform, these young people rallied around the DREAM (Development, Relief, and Education for Alien Minors) Act (first proposed in 2001) as something that could get passed, and they began to use networked communication as a key element of their efforts. The DREAM Act would provide conditional permanent residency to immigrant youth who had attended American high schools and been in residence for at least five years prior to the Bill's enactment. These young activists were in part inspired by the success of the walkouts as proving that young people cared deeply about these issues. Historically, immigrant rights groups have been organized by nationality and ethnicity, whereas the network that formed around the DREAM Act was multi-ethnic, multiracial, and multicultural (Costanza-Chock 2010). Immigrant rights groups have traditionally sought to carefully frame a unified message, whereas the DREAMers sought to multiply the number of voices in the conversation and encourage many young people to tell their own stories through media.

Unfortunately, as it struggled to push its agenda through a lame-duck session of Congress in 2010, the Obama administration was unsuccessful at getting the DREAM Act passed. The young activists then took their struggles to individual states that were considering local versions of the Act. Here, the fact that they were a dispersed, decentralized network made it much easier to coordinate their efforts across different locations. The Obama administration was trying to seem tough on immigration, and it actually deported more people in its first term than the Bush administration did in eight years. The DREAMers called Obama out as the "deporter-in-chief." They adopted a much more confrontational style, exercising various forms of civil disobedience, such as walking into Immigration and Customs Enforcement headquarters in the South and turning themselves in as undocumented and live-streaming the protest until forcibly stopped. Ultimately, Obama blinked. In 2012 he signed off on an executive order that effectively enacted many key provisions of the DREAM Act.

Undocumented youth from the DREAMer movement spoke from the podium at the Democratic National Convention, and their cause was explicitly acknowledged during Obama's second inaugural address. We now know that the Latino vote swung heavily towards Obama in the election. Here, we can see a significant change in public policy largely inspired by youth activism. Yes, they got support from adult activists, but this was very much a youth-led effort, and it yielded substantive results. There were many attempts along the way to block them, but young people proved very adept at routing around the obstacles and continuing to push for what they believed in.

When Arely Zimmerman (2012) interviewed a number of DREAM activists, she found that many of them did not have digital access at home. Many were using school and library computers to connect with their network, and few had formal training using digital tools. They were producing media without expensive cameras – using cell phones, for example. But they developed some important insights into how to use social media for political change. This is consistent with what the Youth and Participatory Politics survey (Cohen and Kahne 2012) discovered: a growing number of minority youth engaged in political activities online. These activities often took forms that looked very different from the tactics associated with previous generations within their communities. For example, they found that more African-American youth had participated in buycotts, directing their consumer power towards specific causes, than boycotts, the archetypical tactic of the civil rights movement. However, there is still heavy stratification on the basis of educational background, and some of the more "advanced" practices here are much more likely to be performed by those with high educational, economic, cultural, and social capital than by those who are more disadvantaged. So, while participatory politics does raise hope for fostering a more democratic culture, it cannot in and of itself overcome structural inequalities that have historically blocked many from participating in civic and political life.

What Counts as Political Participation?

Mimi: Participating in the YPP network has me thinking about the range of what counts as political and civic. The DREAM activist case is important because it does have a dimension of resistance, and is youth driven, but at the end of the day it is about youth mobilizing to create positive alternatives within existing power structures. That feels different from the idea that the only way youth demonstrate being politically aware is by being resistant or anti-authoritarian, by protesting, or by fighting power. It's important to recognize collective action in ways that are youth-driven and generative, but also not just about adult-guided politics or civics.

I've been working with Lissa Soep and Henry's YPP team at USC (Neta Kliger-Vilenchik, Sangita Shresthova, Liana Thompson, and Arely Zimmerman) in thinking through the intersection between connected learning and participatory politics. We've suggested a framework of "connected civics" to describe how educators and young people can strengthen the connections between affinity networks and their civic engagement (Ito et al. 2015). Whether they are DREAM activists or fan activists, networked youth groups are developing connections between their personal passions and civic action. Even though our Leveling Up cases aren't focused explicitly on participatory politics, we see many examples of civic engagement emerging from affinity networks. For example, the StarCraft community organized a StarCraft Without Borders event to raise money for Doctors Without Borders, and anime fans mobilized for disaster relief after the earthquakes and Fukushima nuclear meltdown. These forms of civic and political action have a different cast to them than the kinds of community service or political engagements that have been defined by adults and adult institutions.

Connected civics begins with an appreciation of how young people are developing political and civic capacity when they run their own World of Warcraft guilds, Minecraft servers, or fan conventions, a kind of "little p" politics that contrasts with the more adult-centered "big P" Politics. This kind of organizing may not be about the government, but it is about governance, and it involves trial by fire in experiencing what happens when you have power and authority. It's about having people pissed off at you for how you handled the VIP rooms in the fan convention, or you kickbanning people from an IRC channel. That's where kids are building real capacities that are in the here and now, not about a future when they are adults and able to vote and be full citizens. We hope that connected civics will become a framework through which educators and organizers can build on youth-driven forms of participatory culture and link them more explicitly to civic and political engagement.

Henry: There's been a tendency for political scientists and educators to celebrate participation in student governments as a stepping stone into civic participation (Gibson, Levine et al. 2003). But, if anything, that's a much narrower game where young people exert far less power over their own material conditions than what takes place if a young person becomes a guild leader in World of Warcraft or is running programming for a fan convention, where you make decisions that have consequences for your community. What makes student government a frustrating game is that you know you don't have access to resources and lack the capacity to shape the policies that most directly impact your lives. The school system is never going to allow you to make any kind of significant change. So, you are pretending to be part of a government that gets no say in the governance of the system you're in. A guild leader does get to govern, allocate resources, and lead a community, even if only in a virtual world. Young people are most apt to get excited, to commit themselves fully in activities, where they have a stake, where their efforts have consequences and impact, so we should not be surprised that the current generation of young people is finding these spaces which foster their political voice, as opposed to more traditional kinds of student organizations.

danah: I cannot overemphasize the importance of learning leadership skills. This is important for anyone, including and especially youth. Many young people lack any meaningful form of agency in their lives, and they crave it desperately, especially as they're trying to figure out how they relate to the world around them. Many of the traditional opportunities teens have to show their leadership ability are prescribed for them, so that they act out what adults say it means to be a leader rather than actually learning to lead.

I get really excited when youth challenge the boundaries of their world and find ways to carve out opportunities for leadership and reclaim publics on their own terms. This can take place in unexpected forums. Massively multiplayer online role-playing games (MMORPGs) like World of Warcraft are often dismissed as being fantasy worlds where teens escape, but I see them as spaces where teens can develop a sense of agency and responsibility through their play. In most MMORPG gaming environments, participants must learn how to negotiate productively with people, including strangers. They must develop a sense of when they should take the reins and lead and when it's more productive for them to follow. Those experiences aren't narrated as learning opportunities, but I see them as key for learning civic engagement.

Cultivating Activists and the Harry Potter Alliance

Mimi: The challenge with youth-only or niche worlds is figuring out connections to other sites of power. Otherwise, they don't harness power beyond the specific community. It's important to recognize both the ways in which participatory culture and online worlds develop these kinds of capacities in their participants and that these capacities need to be explicitly organized to have influence in "big P" Politics. It's what the learning world describes as the problem of "transfer" between different contexts. It turns out that even what we think of as general skills like math or reading don't automatically transfer out of a classroom setting to other real-life contexts, or vice versa, unless they are framed as related skills and activities. When we talk to young people in interest communities, they often don't think of what they are doing as "learning" or as "cultivating leadership," even if we might see it in those terms, and they don't think of applying those capacities to school or other adult-oriented areas. Kris Gutiérrez and Barbara Rogoff (2003) talk about this as cultivating "horizontal" expertise as a complement to developing "vertical" or depth knowledge and skills in particular areas.

In YPP, and with connected civics, we talk about building pathways from participatory politics to more traditional or institutionalized forms of political expression and action. Another way of thinking about it has been as a sense of "latent publics," or networks that can be activated for causes, as we saw in the cases of the immigration protests, or when young people mobilized against what they saw as threats to online culture posed by the Stop Online Piracy Act (SOPA) and Preventing Real Online Threats to Economic Creativity and Theft of Intellectual Property Act (PROTECT IP Act, or PIPA) in 2012. We need to create more contexts that enable youth to see their sense of ownership and agency in the youth-driven domain as relevant to an adult-driven domain. That's where examples like the Harry Potter Alliance and other cases coming out of MAPP are so productive, because they give hints as to the kind of vocabulary and cultural frames that can bring those things together.

Henry: The Harry Potter Alliance (HPA) is a vivid example of this process (Kligler-Vilenchik 2013; Kligler-Vilenchik et al. 2012). They start with an empowering fantasy and then link it to real-world concerns – a great example of the civic imagination at work. A generation of young people learned to read through their engagement with the Harry Potter books; they learned to write by creating and sharing Harry Potter fan fiction; and now they are learning how to bring about change by embracing Harry Potter activism. The HPA partners with NGOs and governmental agencies, brokering relationships between fandom and various kinds of political elites. They encourage young people to participate in public policy debates. They have had small-scale but significant success, whether measured in books shipped to Africa, supply planes for Haitian disaster relief, or voters registered to support marriage equality. These kinds of victories allow young participants to make a difference.

Andrew Slack, the HPA founder, has articulated a powerful model for how we might integrate fandom and activism. He inspired me to think back across the history of fandom, which had started in part as a space where young men in the 1930s could actively debate the forces which were changing their society – initially technocratic, but by the depression years incorporating a wider array of ideologies, including socialism (Ross 1991). Some of the first gay rights publications in the United States had been science fiction fanzines (Garber and Paleo 1983), and the emergence of *Star Trek* fandom in the 1960s was closely linked to the emergence of feminist science fiction writers. I wrote in *Textual Poachers* (Jenkins 1992) about Leslie Fish's novel *The Weight*, a vast fan narrative that grew out of her active engagement with anarchist politics. I had already written in *Science Fiction Audiences* (Tulloch and Jenkins 1995) about how the Gaylaxians, a queer science fiction group, led an aggressive letter-writing campaign to get an LGBT character onto *Star Trek: The Next Generation.* The more I looked, the clearer it was that there was a long history of fan activism.

And that legacy is even larger if we broaden it to include moments like the letter-writing campaign in the late 1960s that helped keep *Star Trek* on the air. There have been many such campaigns across the history of fandom. By the time a fan community has organized to protect a favorite show from being canceled, they've identified an issue, found the pressure point in the system, figured out who the key decision-makers are, developed tactics that might influence their decisions, educated others about what they need to do to increase the pressure, and mobilized to take action. Succeed or fail, these fan networks have gone through all of the basic steps necessary to organize a political campaign. But they may well have understood this activity in purely cultural terms and not yet understood its potential political implications. By contrast, the HPA has been very effective at helping participants to map their identities as fans onto their identities as citizens or activists and to organize an effective network committed to ongoing social change.

Mimi: Doing what HPA did requires a layering of relationships, practices, and cultural narratives to help people connect the knowledge and skills from one setting across to another. This gets back to the participation gap. You have to have not only skills and dispositions but also social networks that tie domains together. You have to have a cultural narrative that makes you feel welcome. And you have to have concrete practices and places which link those things. HPA clubs knit together the infrastructure of popular culture with educational practice. What's brilliant about Andrew Slack is that he built connections between cultural and political participation through multiple levers, including narratives that wove together real-world and fantasy-based civic action, and hybrid practices brought civic action into fan events and activities. He created a national infrastructure that sat between popular culture, education, and civics.

This kind of connectivity and transfer happens fairly organically in the geek world. There are lots of hybrid translation zones between fans, geeks, gamers, and coders. It's not that somehow gaming makes you a good coder, necessarily – or that it makes you a remix artist. It's really the fact that, through gaming, conventions, fan sites, and the like, there are these overlapping social networks, practices, identities, and infrastructures that enable that transfer.

danah: I love that you're highlighting the importance of social networks in addition to skills. These are often overlooked, but they're a crucial foundation for people to leverage skills effectively to become activists. A few years back, legal scholar John Palfrey and I were working with Connie Yowell from the MacArthur Foundation to help Lady Gaga and her mother form the Born This Way Foundation to address meanness and cruelty. As part of this project, we dove into the literature and spent a tremendous amount of time spiritedly debating what it would take to empower youth to make change within their communities. We found that many people naïvely assumed that you could say positive things to kids and that this would empower youth to be activists. Empowerment doesn't work this way.

As we were thinking about what knowledge, information, and capacity was necessary to actually empower youth from diverse circumstances to address meanness and cruelty in their communities, we recognized that there were three key pillars: safety, skills, and opportunities. First, youth need to feel strong as individuals. They need to have structural supports for dealing with everything from family difficulties to mental health issues. They also need to have a community to which they can turn for emotional support. These were core to making sure that youth were safe. Next, youth need to develop skills. We talked a lot about "soft" skills, such as social-emotional learning, as well as "hard" skills, such as the ability to make media and communicate messages. Finally, we focused on creating opportunities for diverse youth to use their skills and channel their resilience to make change. We recognized that the kinds of opportunities they needed differed tremendously depending on where they were coming from and how they could envision making change. By looking at the process of empowerment holistically, we were also able to see how different youth are at different stages. What they need to create change in their communities depends significantly on where they're at in their lives. There's no doubt that specific experiences often trigger engagement that can lead to becoming an empowered activist, but people don't simply wake up one day empowered. Activism is cultivated.

Henry: The most effective groups and networks understand the transitional processes which move people from being socially or culturally active in one affinity group towards greater civic and political participation in a wider context. The HPA has also been effective at addressing the politics of self, helping young people to think through everyday life concerns, such as suicide prevention, mental health, and body imagery. It encourages them to come to grips with their own personal identity as well as to commit to changing public policy. Sometimes, the lines between these two levels become very, very murky.

Universal Studios had invited large numbers of fans to the Wizarding World of Harry Potter theme park attraction in Orlando. But the rides are designed so they accommodate only people of a certain size. If you are too "big" – if you are obese or even a bulky guy like a football player

– the ride will not close over you and you cannot ride it safely. Outside the attractions, there was an area where people could see if they would fit in the car. I was there one night which was set aside to celebrate Harry Potter fans, and the result of being "sized" was humiliating within a fan community that's tolerant of people who come in various shapes and sizes. Many fans were very upset. They had traveled a distance; they described visiting this reconstruction of Hogsmeade as a "homecoming" to the space of their fantasy. Some of them were being locked out of participating in the experience because someone thought they weren't the right size. This inspired activism around body image. How do you see yourself? Do you hate your body? How do we deal with childhood obesity? The flipside was: how might fans put pressure on Universal Studios to change the design of its park so that it is actually more accommodating of people of diverse size?

The genius of the organizations is that they could draw connections across all of these levels – the themes of the Harry Potter novels, the real-world experiences and self-images of fans, the economics of running theme parks, and "capital P" political issues. Fan activism starts where people live – within communities where they have a sense of safety and security, where they have a collective identity and shared culture, and where there is a set of ideals and commitments, even a set of networks, cultural practices, and ways of doing things. You build out from there mechanisms for civic learning and political mobilization.

The HPA is not a single-issue organization. It mobilizes around an evolving set of concerns, with the young participants helping to identify causes and tactics through their involvement in both local and national networks of fan activists. There are always new opportunities for different kids with different values, commitments, and concerns to connect with the organization and direct its attention towards a new struggle. And these activities operate on a range of levels – from self-expression and self-empowerment to what we might traditionally describe as charity activities (book drives, disaster relief), to voter registration drives, to more contentious forms of advocacy (such as struggles over free trade practices or support for minimum-wage workers). Their activities allow young people to use the skills they have acquired as fans to make a difference in the world – and never ask that they renounce their identities as fans.

Mimi: HPA has definitely been a good case for us to study in terms of how to build pathways between youth-centered and popular practices and more adult-centered and political areas. The big challenge for us is to see if this model can work in relation to other popular cultural forms and other demographics. The Harry Potter fandom is close to home in terms of the kinds of participatory cultures with which academics feel affinity – white, intellectual, geek leaning. I think some of the other cases we are looking at in the YPP project, as well as in the Connected Learning Research Network, stretch us a bit beyond this comfortable home base. For example, Crystle Martin in my team is doing a case study around learning and professional wrestling. Rachel Cody is studying the civic activism of the community of knitters and crocheters of ravelry.com. The degree to which we can see these models derived from such exemplary cases as HPA in other kinds of interest, identities, and demographics will be the real test as to whether these practices can extend beyond already engaged youth. In MAPP, the cases of libertarian youth, DREAMers, Invisible Children, and American Muslim youth are important steps in this direction.

Spreading Change: *Kony 2012*, It Gets Better, and 4chan

Henry: Looking across these cases has helped us to understand the range of activist strategies that are being mobilized through participatory culture. One of the things that experience within participatory culture provides these young activists is an understanding of how to get attention for their causes and how to circulate content effectively so that it reaches the right people and enters larger conversations. Some of this has to do with media production capacity. The HPA uses video blogs to frame and circulate its messages, and the same is true of most of the other groups we study. Sometimes these videos circulate among the supporters. The DREAMers talk, for example, about how hard it is to identify and join forces with other undocumented youth, and videos about "coming out" as undocumented helped them to identify common issues and concerns and simply to find each other. At the same time, though, most Americans have never met anyone they knew was undocumented, and when people encountered these videos via YouTube, it changed the ways they thought about the issues. So, these videos serve both bonding functions – connecting supporters with each other – and bridging functions – establishing contact with other communities that might be allies to their cause.

I am fascinated with the role of the superhero myth among DREAMers. In the summer of 2011, Superman renounced his American citizenship, declaring he would no longer be fighting just for the "American way" but would be fighting for global justice. Although this event occurred in an alternative-universe story with a DC comic book and did not affect the main continuity of the Superman saga, conservative radio hosts and political leaders were outraged at this idea, calling it unpatriotic. But the DREAM activists asked, "When did Superman ever become an American citizen?" If ever there was an "illegal alien," it is Kal-El of Krypton, whose parents sent him to another world in search of a better life, who crosses the border in the middle of the night, lands outside Smallville, and gets adopted by an Anglo family. He masks his true identity, living in hiding for the rest of his life. He is nevertheless generous enough to serve the American public, despite the fact that he is never really able to call himself an American. This reframing turns out to be a really effective way to deconstruct and rewrite the Superman myth. It shakes up the ways people think about the immigrant experience, allowing them to attach the struggle for immigrant rights to a narrative many of us are already invested in. It also links our current struggle for undocumented youth to a larger history of immigration in America. Superman's story was created by two first-generation Eastern European high-school students in Cleveland, Ohio. Superman was from the start a classic immigrant narrative, and the DREAMers are reclaiming those associations across seventy years of cultural history.

danah: Reframing is a really powerful tactic, especially when it allows people to recognize their own assumptions and biases and question the things that they take for granted. I was doing fieldwork in 2006 when Dove released the 60-second "Evolution" video as part of their "Real Beauty" campaign. This video showed how an attractive but fairly normal looking white woman was transformed into an ideal model through makeup and Photoshop. This video was posted to YouTube and teens forwarded it to their friends. Many had never stopped to think about why the pictures they saw on the newsstands didn't look like anyone that they had ever met. While they did not make the video themselves, teen girls played an important role in spreading a message about the artificial nature of beauty culture in the United States.

Henry: This is what happened – on perhaps a horrific scale – with Invisible Children's *Kony 2012* campaign. Circulated primarily via YouTube, this video sought to direct public attention and advocate military action against a Ugandan warlord, Joseph Kony, who was kidnapping children and forcing them to serve in his paramilitary organization. IC proved very effective at creating spreadable media – media that circulated widely across the web – but they were less effective at building drillability – the capacity of people to drill down and develop a more in-depth understanding of the issues. *Kony 2012* was not an overnight success. IC had spent more than a decade recruiting and training members, framing issues, and trying out different strategies and tactics (Kligler-Vilenchik and Shresthova 2012). They had built a network of supporters in clubs organized at schools and churches across the country who could spread the video and amplify its message.

Kony 2012 hit a critical inflection point. Based on their previous experience, IC leaders had estimated internally that the video might reach half a million viewers during the two months they planned to run their campaign. Instead, it was seen by more than 70 million people in its first four days of circulation, becoming what was up until that time the fastest-moving and most widely circulated video in the history of YouTube. This is several times the number of people who saw the highest rated show on American television (*Modern Family*) and the highest grossing film at the box office (*Hunger Games*) that week. This example suggested that, at least some of the time, the circulation of grassroots media can overwhelm the capacity of traditional media. This success completely swamped the organization's capacity to respond.

Some of the criticism directed against *Kony 2012* was legitimate; some of it was based on misunderstandings that resulted from this recontextualization of the content. A message intended for mostly internal audiences went global, reaching many people who had not taken part in the organization's previous conversations. Some of the concerns critics felt were missing from *Kony 2012* were part of other videos IC had produced.

As the video spread to new audiences, and as the leadership was confronting internal challenges (including the highly publicized nervous breakdown of their spokesperson), the young people who had passed the video along through their social networks were forced to confront these critiques on their own, without access to adequate information, without any real training or experience in the skills of rebuttal. They were not in a position to defend the *Kony 2012* effort, and they felt crushed by what unfolded in its aftermath. Some of this was a consequence of a highly centralized leadership meeting a highly decentralized network, but many young people got caught in the crossfire as IC came under attack from more established activist organizations, policy think tanks, editorialists, and political leaders. IC lost control of its message, and young people were the ones on the ground who lost face with their friends when they couldn't explain what was going on.

danah: From my perspective, the *Kony 2012* phenomenon highlighted how social media is only valuable once existing networks have been put into place. After the so-called viral spread of the video, my partner Gilad Lotan (2012) decided to analyze the #kony2012 hashtag on Twitter to understand how it popped so quickly. In looking at the network of those who posted on this topic, he saw something peculiar. There were all of these seemingly disconnected subgraphs that appeared to be tight-knit friend groups of young people located in smaller conservative American cities like Birmingham and Oklahoma City. When he analyzed the profiles of the posters, he noticed a startling trend in the words they referenced in their bios: the repetition of "Jesus," "God," and "Christ" were particularly illuminating. Through some investigation, we realized that Invisible Children had been touring churches for quite some time, building up a broad network of people whom they could activate. Sure enough, when they launched *Kony 2012*, that's exactly what they did. They asked their network to tweet and they did. Because it looked like thousands of disconnected Twitter users suddenly started talking about one thing, the hashtag quickly trended, which helped it spread further. This wasn't a grassroots youth-generated phenomenon, but initially it looked that way. Of course, just because Invisible Children had created a network structure that made popularizing a hashtag viable didn't mean that they had a sustained mechanism to keep engaging activated people. And the failure of communication and coordination definitely took a toll when the critics started in.

Henry: Invisible Children did have some strong grassroots elements through those chapters you are identifying. My team had been following the group closely for two years before *Kony 2012* hit the national radar. We saw the various ways they had recruited and trained those young activists, helping them to construct and share their own stories of concern about the issue and building up their capacity to act behind a broad range of causes. Many of them felt a strong ownership of the IC message, even if there were also strong top-down dimensions in how it was constructed. Ironically, the success of *Kony 2012* (and the painful aftermath) has meant that IC has gradually pulled away from building up the grassroots capacities of its participants, first moved towards a more centralized and authority-based structure within the organization, and finally discontinued most of its outreach to youth altogether. IC has announced it is dismantling all US operations by the end of

2015. We've seen the young people themselves move onto a range of other causes and movements, taking with them experiences, skills, knowledge, and values they learned through their involvement in IC. Just as it is easy on the surface to see the group as a fully grassroots movement, the reaction after *Kony 2012* has tended to underestimate the grassroots dimensions of its operations at the time.

danah: On the one hand, it's exciting to see youth play a central role in a global media phenomenon – and many youth who were a part of the *Kony 2012* project felt seriously empowered. On the other, it's a bit troublesome to watch youth be used uncritically to amplify a message. I am especially worried about youth becoming part of a media messaging machine because of what happened with the "It Gets Better" campaign.

At first blush, "It Gets Better" seems like a brilliant campaign. Started by Dan Savage and his partner, it involves countless inspiring videos of LGBTQ-identified individuals and their allies talking about issues of inequality and injustice, highlighting their own stories and speaking to younger generations about how it gets better. Many teenagers also decided to make videos to contribute to this phenomenon. Unfortunately, though, participation in the phenomenon was not equivalent to participation in a community. Many of these youth found that putting up an "It Gets Better" video made them more vulnerable to teasing and harassment at school. And, since there was no one in the movement to turn to, the impact of creating a video ended up putting some youth in a worse place. My heart hit the floor when I started hearing of deaths by suicide by LGBTQ-identified youth who had made videos. I think it's important to recognize that being a part of a participatory culture movement does not necessarily mean being a part of a participatory culture community. This goes back to my belief that youth need to be safe first; that includes making sure that they have structural supports and interpersonal networks to keep them strong.

Henry: I agree. I think that there's a tendency among writers discussing activism to dismiss the importance of this idea of a safe space – a zone where young people can find their footing as citizens and activists before they are shoved into confrontation with other opposing forces. This need for a safe space is especially true for youth who may not have a strong sense of safety in other aspects of their lives – who may not yet feel secure in their social identities, say, or who may confront hostile conditions in their schools and homes to begin with.

Writers such as Malcolm Gladwell (2010) reflect a wider tendency to dismiss the social risks that young activists are taking. For example, the tactic of changing one's social media profile picture to support marriage equality often gets described as the most minimal form of political action. Yet I suspect for a teenage girl in Smyrna, Georgia, where she lives surrounded by homophobic discourse and practice, there is more than a little risk in coming out in support of same-sex marriage, especially in a forum where your statement is visible, indiscriminately, to classmates, parents, folks from your church, and so forth. What's on the screen is simply a representation of the many kinds of in-person exchanges she's apt to have over the coming week as people question her choice to embrace this collective symbolic action. She is likely to experience the consequences of her political speech on the ground, in the context of her everyday transactions, where she lives. Yet these young people are also not simply exposed; as people choose to make support for marriage equality part of their social identity, they are also able to discover others within their network who share their values and are ready to stake out the same position. Their individual expressions become part of a larger network, which may provide them with some of the support they need to take the next steps (though, as danah demonstrates, there's no guarantee that this social structure will be in place for them without conscious effort to build a community).

danah: Another interesting network-enabled community to consider in light of political activism is 4chan. For the most part, participation in 4chan is "for the lulz" – entertainment, often at someone else's expense – but things got serious a few years ago when a group of people born out of 4chan started calling themselves Anonymous as they critically attacked Scientology for having too much power (Coleman 2014). Needless to say, the political actions of Anonymous took on new light when members of the fragmented network started defending WikiLeaks and the actions of hackers against American corporations and the US government. Anonymous continues to engage in a plethora of different "operations," targeting child pornographers and drug cartels as well as government agencies and commercial entities that they deem corrupt.

Not all of Anonymous – or 4chan – is comprised of youth, but many young people are deeply involved in those networks. Through their engagement there, they're learning how to be political and how to achieve political goals. It's easy to be critical of 4chan and Anonymous – as many governments are – but countless young people are challenging the status quo through their participation in these loose networks of self-identified "freedom fighters." Their coordinated, networked, and anarchic form of demanding change is completely off-putting both to traditional activists and to those in power, but I think that, in them, we're seeing new forms of activism emerge.

The form of activism embodied by 4chan, Anonymous, and loose networks of hackers is very much rooted in the technological capacity of the new systems that exist. As such, the politics and practices that unfold are foreign (and thus terrifying) to many, while offering a new way of thinking and acting for many activists. This is not without huge challenges and complications. For all of the productive interventions that have occurred, there are also acts that challenge our society's understanding of acceptable mechanisms of change. And, thus, we see a lot of powerful actors starting to clamp down on activists engaged in nouveau technologically mediated political acts.

It's also important to keep in mind that, while people use technology to challenge power structures, networked technologies are complicating how power is negotiated. In *Communication Power*, Manuel Castells (2011) argues that power resides in those who can control the social, technical, political, economic, and information networks that are central to contemporary society. He sees technological innovation as productive and disruptive but not necessarily as the game changer that tech utopians might envision. From his perspective, the introduction and uptake of new technologies destabilizes the status quo, forcing a scramble for power. Those who already have access to power or are otherwise quite privileged are most likely to reclaim power during these destabilizing moments. But these points of instability create openings for new players too. And so, in the scramble for power, new voices also enter the field. Many of the examples we've discussed reveal how this can unfold, but there's also a tidal wave happening where old systems of power are working very hard to reclaim power and clamp down on the new voices that have emerged.

Henry: For me, this discussion circles back around to the question of who gets to decide what counts as politics. We began this discussion with Fiske's (1989) comments about the Madonna fan who discovers her own voice through cultural participation, who forges a collective identity and learns to express her shared concerns in conversation with other young women. For many, this activity did not look like politics, just as some of the activities that Connected Learning researchers have examined did not necessarily look like traditional education. When this same generation of young women deployed their zines and, later, their home pages to claim an identity as "third-wave feminists," more people seemed ready to recognize what they were doing as having a political impact, even if that impact was not necessarily directed at the realm of institutionalized politics, like winning elections or passing laws. As Ethan Zuckerman (2013) has noted, these forms of institutionalized practice represent only one axis along which political change might take place.

As we map our case studies, we see some of the groups my MAPP team is studying define success in very traditional terms: The DREAMer movement wants to pass legislation or otherwise shape federal immigration policy. Some of them seek to support or influence NGOs and other kinds of organizations or to raise awareness and shape the public perceptions of an issue. Some want to change the way we behave towards each other, as is often the case at the early stages of movements for equality or tolerance, such as the efforts of American Muslim youth to change the ways they are perceived in a post-9/11 America.

Some may also seek to change the ways we construct our identities and feel about ourselves, as in movements around body image or sexual identity. Some, such as the next wave of young libertarians, prefer to promote change through education rather than working within governmental or institutional structures.

For some of these tasks, young people need to work in concert with adults and thus need to adopt a language that translates easily between the realm of participatory politics and the realm of institutional politics. For others, what's important is their ability to communicate among themselves, so they may use language that seems, from the perspective of adult gatekeepers, informal, irreverent, even salty. These authorities are too quick to dismiss such activities and languages as inappropriate or trivial forms of political participation. At the same time, young people are reluctant to label what they are doing as politics or activism, because these terms carry such negative connotations, especially in an era defined by partisan impasse. Youth see themselves as exerting change at a cultural rather than an institutional level. We need to learn to recognize and respect this as politics by another means.

Chapter 7

Reimagining Participatory Culture

By danah boyd, Mimi Ito, and Henry Jenkins

This book documents a shared process of reflection and conversation about how the concept of participatory culture has evolved, devolved, and been refined through the years. Through the lens of participatory culture, we have taken stock of our ongoing research, our personal investments, and our challenges and aspirations as public intellectuals.

Two decades ago, we were excited by the expanded access to communication capabilities that were impacting the everyday lives of many people around the world. Today, we are also struck by how many people are still not able to participate meaningfully, how many are cut off from the kinds of cultural, political, and educational possibilities we have been describing. Again and again, this conversation has centered on issues of inequality and exclusion because, while we may live in a more participatory culture, we do not yet live in a fully participatory culture. Participatory culture is by its very nature a work in progress, as are our ongoing agendas for research and social change. That said, we would like to conclude by reflecting on some of the shared values, perspectives, and commitments that have emerged through our dialogue and collaborative writing.

Core Values

Each of us was initially drawn to the concept of participatory culture for two reasons: first, our connections with fandom, geek culture, or various subcultural identities were such a large part of our own lives and, second, these groups were among the early adopters and adapters of new media. They were among the first to experiment with the ways that, say, communities of interests or networked publics might deploy the affordances of early digital and mobile technologies. As the populations using these platforms have diversified, and as these technologies have become more mainstream, our perspectives have evolved. On the one hand, we have seen a diversification of participatory uses of these technologies and, on the other, we are seeing the stripping away of the subcultural politics that once informed our relationship to the online world. The first set of developments (diversification) makes it harder to describe the commonalities between different kinds of participatory culture. The second (mainstreaming) makes it harder to identify what's transformative about participatory culture. Participatory culture risks being both everything and nothing. For this reason, we need a more refined vocabulary for distinguishing between competing models of participation, especially at a time when the rhetoric of participation gets deployed by institutions which have done little or nothing to broaden who gets to participate or what power they are willing to cede to participants.

As a set of ideals, we can define participatory culture in opposition to various forms of culture that limit access to the means of cultural production and circulation, that fragment and isolate the public rather than providing opportunities to create and share culture, and that construct hierarchies that make it difficult for many to exert any meaningful influence over the core decisions that impact their lives. People participate through and within communities: participatory culture requires us to move beyond a focus on individualized personal expression; it is about an ethos of "doing it together" in addition to "doing it yourself." Many of the cases we often use to illustrate the concept fall short of these ideals. Such examples do not discredit our hopes for a more participatory culture, but they do force us continually to revisit and reappraise what counts as meaningful participation.

In an ideal setting, anyone could come to the table and be treated equally. But, for this to work, all individuals would need to have equal power and agency. While achieving such systemic equality is certainly desirable, we're not so naïve as to think that such a truly participatory culture is going to emerge anytime soon. The world is rife with structural inequities and differential power; while it's critical to challenge and combat such inequalities, they are not going to disappear – certainly not without sustained struggle. Yet, our goal should be to continually create contexts that are more participatory than before. In other words, participatory culture is not about creating a particular state of society, but about collectively engaging in an aspirational project that constantly challenges us to expand opportunities for meaningful participation.

Political Orientation

No single ideological orientation (left, right, or center) has a monopoly on the virtues of a more participatory culture. We see communities and individuals across the political spectrum embracing its practices and values. People often implicitly associate participatory culture with progressive politics, but many conservative groups are founded on values of expanded communicative capacity, encourage grassroots mobilization, and embrace contributions from those who have not historically had access to power. At the same time, much as Stephen Johnson (2012) has defined the notion of "peer progressivism," we do feel participatory culture has a politicized vision of the world in which more people have access to the means of knowledge and cultural production and have a voice in governance and collective action. Of course, this belief also may stem from our own political biases. All three of us are progressive and deeply committed to democratic ideals. Thus, our instincts are often to look at, engage with, and participate in progressive constructions of participatory culture, even though more conservative incarnations do exist.

Like internet culture, participatory culture has countercultural and anti-authoritarian valences reflecting its roots, but it is also increasingly intertwined with commercial and capitalist forms of cultural and technological production. The orientation towards collective action and peer-to-peer sharing sits uneasily next to values of individual freedom and autonomy. As internet culture has become increasingly global, Euro-American labels become even more inadequate to describe the political terrain of participatory culture.

Both Descriptive and Aspirational

Participatory culture can be and has been used both as a descriptive model and as an aspirational one. As a descriptive model, it indicates a set of practices that have centered on accessible and communal forms of cultural production and sharing. As an aspirational model, it embodies a set of ideals for how these social practices can facilitate learning, empowerment, civic action, and capacity-building. When we look at specific practices, such as discussing issues in online forums, creating a Makerbot, joining a Facebook cause, or uploading a video on YouTube for one's online community, it's not always clear whether the practice can be flagged as part of participatory culture, because it's not always clear whether the practice satisfies the aspirational values of participatory culture.

There have been moves to refine our definitions of participatory culture. Nico Carpentier (2011), for example, has proposed that the term "participation" be reserved only for those cases where all actors in a decision-making process operate from a position of equal power and status. For Carpentier, this definition is aspirational and rarely achieved in practice; it's a set of goals he feels we should be working towards. Rather than draw this line in the sand, we feel it's more productive to view the term as relational in nature.

For us, participation is not an absolute: it's defined in opposition to the dominant structures of institutionalized power. In the 1980s, it was about fans resisting and appropriating forms of commercial media. Today, it is about people finding voice, agency, and collective intelligence within the corporate-maintained structures of Web 2.0 platforms.

Participation is about People

Participatory culture is not contained within a platform or set of technological features, whether Facebook, Twitter, conventions, or self-published zines. Rather, it is about a set of practices embedded in shared norms and values. At times, these practices manifest in particular technologies, and, quite often, those invested in participatory culture leverage existing platforms to serve their goals, but participation should be understood in socio-cultural rather than technological terms.

Critics of participatory culture often highlight the ways in which new technologies reinscribe existing structural inequalities. We recognize that this is true, but we don't believe that technologies determine outcomes, whether positive or negative. Technologies do mirror and magnify many aspects of society – good, bad, and ugly. The technologies do not themselves make culture participatory. People do. And they do so by imagining – and working to achieve – new ways of connecting, coordinating, collaborating, and creating.

Participatory culture is also not simply the product of a cultural consciousness-raising brought about by the rise of new media. Many of the practices that we're identifying are historically resilient practices inflected by today's media in new ways. Yet, there is an important twist brought about by social media in particular. Through these new media contexts, we can observe a set of practices that, more often than not, were historically difficult to identify and track. The very nature of networked publics – the persistence of interactions, the spreadability of media, and the searchability of content – makes it easier to see participatory culture in action. This visibility is also why it's often hard to untangle participatory culture from new media. On the one hand, this new visibility increases the impact of participatory practices, expanding their reach and scope, and accelerating their circulation. On the other, this new visibility leaves these groups and practices more susceptible to surveillance from governmental and corporate bodies that might wish to limit or regulate participation towards their own ends.

Relation to Capital

Because of the entanglement between participatory culture and technological practices – and because participatory culture gained broad traction as a concept alongside the rise of social media – there is often conceptual slippage between participatory culture and Web 2.0. Web 2.0 is itself an amorphous idea onto which people project their own conceptual anxieties and concerns. When people reject participatory culture because of concerns about Web 2.0, they are typically referring to the perceived agendas of the contemporary venture capitalists and entrepreneurs in Silicon Valley. In essence, participatory culture is rejected as being a justification for American capitalism.

There is little doubt that many corporations have grabbed hold of different aspects of participatory culture in an effort to control, channel, and commodify such activities. Likewise, social media companies – driven by a model of advertising that relies on large quantities of data – are profiting from participatory culture practices taking root inside their ecosystem. But this does not mean that participatory culture is simply beholden to capitalist agendas. Some parts of participatory culture are quite resistant to capitalism. Other aspects are less critical and, perhaps, some may be more heavily shaped by corporate logics.

We cannot untether participatory culture from corporate interests because participatory culture is not happening in a void. While we believe that the corporate dimensions should be critiqued, we also believe that participatory culture should not be thrown out simply because its practices and values do not protect us from the ills of neo-liberal capitalism.

An Evolving Concept

All of this is to say that our understanding of participatory culture should not be static. Rather, we should see participatory culture as an evolving concept that always gets read in relation to existing practices and norms. With each step towards a more participatory culture, we are also raising the stakes and upping the standards by which we evaluate our actual practices. What we might describe as a "participatory turn" is partially in response to decades-long debates about cultural and political participation and partially about rising expectations concerning the affordances of new media. Each shift in our material reality allows us to imagine new possibilities for change. We know that, historically, revolutions occur not when conditions are at their worst but, rather, when conditions are improving and when newly enfranchised groups start to develop a shared vision of what a better society might look like. The same may be the case with participatory culture. A rhetoric of participation raises expectations and often forms the basis of more active resistance to constraints that might have seemed acceptable under other circumstances. No wonder so many Web 2.0 companies have been the focus of debates around privacy and data-mining, copyright and intellectual property, branding practices, and many other elements of their terms of service. The rhetoric of Web 2.0 had promised an easy melding of the interests of producers and consumers. But these relations were always going to be the focus of struggles, with incremental victories and losses, as we fought for the terms of our participation in what many hoped would be a more inclusive and empowered culture.

This book has been a conversation between scholars of different generations and different disciplinary backgrounds who have come together to work on shared projects and who have found themselves addressing similar sets of questions. We hope that it will inspire further conversations within and between groups of educators, policy-makers, scholars, concerned citizens, industry insiders, fans, and anyone else who is concerned about the future of our culture. Insofar as the ideals of participatory culture depend upon processes of collective deliberation and shared reflection, then our theories should emerge in as open and collaborative a manner as possible. We need to be talking this through with a range of other stakeholders, who may contest promises of greater participation based on their own diverse experiences, values, and knowledge. We hope you will follow our example, gather friends, collaborators and critics, students and strangers, and talk through the issues surrounding our current moment of media change.

References

Altman, Rick (1999) *Film/Genre*. London: British Film Institute.

Ananny, Mike (2011) "The Curious Connection between Apps for Gay Men and Sex Offenders," *The Atlantic*, 14 April, www.theatlantic.com/technology/archive/2011/04/the-curious-connection-between-apps-for-gay-men-and-sex-offenders/237340/.

Banet-Weiser, Sarah (2012) *Authentic™: The Politics of Ambivalence in a Brand Culture*. New York: New York University Press.

Bazelon, Emily (2013) *Sticks and Stones: Defeating the Culture of Bullying and Rediscovering the Power of Character and Empathy*. New York: Random House.

Benkler, Yochai (2007) *The Wealth of Networks*. New Haven, CT: Yale University Press.

Bennett, Andy, and Keith Kahn-Harris, eds (2004) *After Subculture: Critical Studies in Contemporary Youth Culture*. New York: Palgrave Macmillan.

Bernays, Edward L. ([1928] 2005) *Propaganda*. Brooklyn, NY: Ig.

Bijker, Wiebe E., Thomas P. Hughes, and Trevor J. Pinch, eds (1987) *The Social Construction of Technological Systems: New Directions in the Sociology and History of Technology*. Cambridge, MA: MIT Press.

Black, Rebecca W. (2008) *Adolescence and Online Fan Fiction*. New York: Peter Lang.

Bodroghkozy, Aniko (2012) *Equal Time: Television and the Civil Rights Movement*. Urbana: University of Illinois Press.

boyd, danah (2011) "White Flight in Networked Publics? How Race and Class Shaped American Teen Engagement with MySpace and Facebook," pp. 203–22 in *Race After the Internet*, ed. Lisa Nakamura and Peter Chow-White. New York: Routledge.

boyd, danah (2014) *It's Complicated: The Social Lives of Networked Teens*. New Haven, CT: Yale University Press.

boyd, danah, and Kate Crawford (2012) "Critical Questions for Big Data: Provocations for a Cultural, Technological, and Scholarly Phenomenon," *Information, Communication, & Society* 15(5): 662–79.

boyd, danah, and Eszter Hargittai (2013) "Connected and Concerned: How Parental Concerns about Online Safety Issues Vary," *Policy & Internet* 5(3): 245–69.

Brown, John Seely, Allan Collins, and Paul Duguid (1989) "Situated Cognition and the Culture of Learning," *Educational Researcher* 18: 32–7.

Buckingham, David (2003) *Media Education: Literacy, Learning, and Contemporary Culture*. Cambridge: Polity.

Burgess, Jean, and Joshua Green (2009) *YouTube: Online Video and Participatory Culture*. Cambridge: Polity.

Carfagna, Lindsey B. (2014) *Beyond Learning-as-Usual: Connected Learning among Open Learners*. Irvine, CA: Digital Media and Learning Research Hub.

Carfagna, Lindsey B., Emilie A. Dubois, Connor Fitzmaurice, Monique Y. Ouimette, Juliet B. Schor, and Margaret Willis (2014) "An Emerging Eco-Habitus: The Reconfiguration of High Cultural Capital Practices among Ethical Consumers," *Journal of Consumer Culture* 14(2): 158–78.

Carpentier, Nico (2011) *Media and Participation: A Site of Ideological-Democratic Struggle*. Bristol: Intellect.

Cassell, Justine, and Meg Cramer (2008) "High Tech or High Risk: Moral Panics about Girls Online," pp. 53–76 in *Digital Youth, Innovation, and the Unexpected*, ed. Tara McPherson. Cambridge, MA: MIT Press.

Castells, Manuel (2011) *Communication Power.* New York: Oxford University Press.

Cherny, Lynn, and Elizabeth Reba Weise, eds (1996) *Wired Women: Gender and New Realities in Cyberspace.* Emeryville, CA: Seal.

Clark, Lynn Scofield (2012) *The Parent App: Understanding Families in the Digital Age.* New York: Oxford University Press.

Cohen, Cathy J., and Joseph Kahne (2012) *Participatory Politics: New Media and Youth Political Action.* Chicago: MacArthur Foundation.

Cole, Michael (1998) "Can Cultural Psychology Help Us Think about Diversity?" *Mind, Culture, and Activity* 5(4): 291–304.

Coleman, Gabriella (2013) *Coding Freedom: The Ethics and Aesthetics of Hacking.* Princeton, NJ: Princeton University Press.

Coleman, Gabriella (2014) *Hacker, Hoaxer, Whistleblower, Spy: The Many Faces of Anonymous.* New York: Verso.

Costanza-Chock, Sasha (2010) *Se ve, se siente: Transmedia Mobilization in the Los Angeles Immigrant Rights Movement.* Los Angeles: University of Southern California [dissertation].

Costanza-Chock, Sasha (2014) *Out of the Shadows, Into the Streets! Transmedia Organizing and the Immigrant Rights Movement.* Cambridge, MA: MIT Press.

Cuban, Larry (1986) *Teachers and Machines: The Classroom Use of Technology since 1920.* New York: Teachers College Press.

Cuban, Larry (2009) *The Blackboard and the Bottom Line: Why Schools Can't Be Businesses.* Cambridge, MA: Harvard University Press.

De Kosnik, Abigail (2013) "Interrogating 'Free' Fan Labor," in *Spreadable Media*, ed. Henry Jenkins, Sam Ford, and Joshua Green. New York: New York University Press; available at http://spreadablemedia.org/essays/kosnik/.

DuBois, Emilie A., Juliet B. Schor, and Lindsey B. Carfagna (2014) "New Cultures of Connection in a Boston Time Bank," pp. 95–124 in *Sustainable Lifestyles and the Quest for Plenitude: Case Studies of the New Economy*, ed. Juliet B. Schor and Craig J. Thompson. New Haven, CT: Yale University Press.

Eckert, Penny (1989) *Jocks and Burnouts*. New York: Teachers College Press.

Ellison, Nicole, and danah boyd (2013) "Sociality through Social Network Sites," pp. 151–72 in *The Oxford Handbook of Internet Studies*, ed. William H. Dutton. Oxford: Oxford University Press.

Engeström, Yrjö, Reijo Miettinen, and Raija-Leena Punamäki, eds (1999) *Perspectives on Activity Theory*. Cambridge: Cambridge University Press.

Epstein, Dmitry, Erik C. Nisbet, and Tarleton Gillespie (2011) "Who's Responsible for the Digital Divide? Public Perceptions and Policy Implications," *Information Society* 27(2): 92–104.

Fake, Caterina (2011) "FOMO and Social Media," http://caterina. net/2011/03/15/fomo-and-social-media/.

Fiske, John (1989) *Reading the Popular*. London: Routledge.

Gamber Thompson, Liana (2012) "The Cost of Engagement: Politics and Participatory Practices in the U.S. Liberty Movement," Youth and Participatory Politics Network, http://ypp.dmlcentral.net/publications/106.

Garber, Eric, and Lin Paleo (1983) *Uranian Worlds: A Reader's Guide to Alternative Sexuality in Science Fiction and Fantasy*. Boston: G. K. Hall.

Gibson, Cynthia, Peter Levine et al. (2003) *The Civic Mission of Schools*. Center for Information & Research on Civic Learning and Engagement, www.civicyouth.org/special-report-the-civic-mission-of-schools/.

Giles, Jim (2005) "Special Report: Internet Encyclopedias Go Head to Head," *Nature* 438: 900–1.

Gillespie, Tarleton (2014) "The Relevance of Algorithms," pp. 167–94 in *Media Technologies*, ed. Tarleton Gillespie, Pablo Boczkowski, and Kirsten Foot. Cambridge, MA: MIT Press; available at http://culture digitally.org/2012/11/the-relevance-of-algorithms/.

Gladwell, Malcolm (2010) "Small Change: Why the Revolution Will

Not Be Tweeted," *New Yorker*, October 4, www.newyorker.com/reporting/2010/10/04/101004fa_fact_gladwell.

Goldman, Shelley, and Raymond McDermott (1987) "The Culture of Competition in American Schools," pp. 282–300 in *Education and Cultural Process: Anthropological Approaches,* ed. George Spindler. 2nd edn, Prospect Heights, IL: Waveland Press.

Gray, Mary L. (2009) *Out in the Country: Youth, Media and Queer Visibility in Rural America.* New York: New York University Press.

Greeno, James G. (1998) "The Situativity of Knowing, Learning, and Research," *American Psychologist* 53(1): 5–17.

Gutiérrez, Kris, and Barbara Rogoff (2003) "Cultural Ways of Learning: Individual Traits or Repertoires of Practice," *Educational Researcher* 32(5): 19–25.

Gutiérrez, Kris D., P. Zitlali Morales, and Danny C. Martinez (2009) "Re-mediating Literacy: Culture, Difference, and Learning for Students from Nondominant Communities," *Review of Research in Education* 33(1): 213–45.

Hall, G. Stanley (1908) *Adolescence.* London: Appleton.

Hall, Stuart (1981) "Notes on Deconstructing 'The Popular,'" pp. 227–40 in *People's History and Socialist Theory*, ed. Raphael Samuel. London: Routledge & Kegan Paul.

Hall, Stuart, and Tony Jefferson, eds (1993) *Resistance through Rituals: Youth Cultures in Post-War Britain.* London: Routledge.

Hargittai, Eszter (2010) "Digital Na(t)ives? Variation in Internet Skills and Uses among Members of the 'Net Generation,'" *Sociological Inquiry* 80: 92–113.

Harris-Lacewell, Melissa Victoria (2006) *Barbershops, Bibles, and BET: Everyday Talk and Black Political Thought.* Princeton, NJ: Princeton University Press.

Hebdidge, Dick (1979) *Subculture: The Meaning of Style.* London: Routledge.

Hine, Thomas (1999) *The Rise and Fall of the American Teenager.* New York: Perennial.

Hodkinson, Paul (2002) *Goth: Identity, Style and Subculture*. Oxford: Berg.

Hoover, Stewart M., Lynn Schofield Clark, and Diane F. Alters (2003) *Media, Home and Family*. New York: Routledge.

Hutchins, Edwin (1995) *Cognition in the Wild*. Cambridge, MA: MIT Press.

Ito, Mizuko (2009) *Engineering Play*. Cambridge, MA: MIT Press.

Ito, Mizuko (2012a) "'As Long as it's Not Linkin Park Z': Popularity, Distinction, and Status in the AMV Subculture," pp. 275–98 in *Fandom Unbound: Otaku Culture in a Connected World*, ed. Mizuko Ito, Daisuke Okabe, and Izumi Tsuji. New Haven, CT: Yale University Press.

Ito, Mizuko (2012b) "Contributors v. Leechers: Fansubbing Ethics and a Hybrid Public Culture," pp. 179–204 in *Fandom Unbound: Otaku Culture in a Connected World*, ed. Mizuko Ito, Daisuke Okabe, and Izumi Tsuji. New Haven, CT: Yale University Press.

Ito, Mizuko, and Daisuke Okabe (2005) "Technosocial Situations: Emergent Structurings of Mobile Email Use," pp. 257–73 in *Personal, Portable, Pedestrian: Mobile Phones in Japanese Life*, ed. Mizuko Ito, Daisuke Okabe, and Misa Matsuda. Cambridge, MA: MIT Press.

Ito, Mizuko, Daisuke Okabe, and Misa Matsuda, eds (2005) *Personal, Portable, Pedestrian: Mobile Phones in Japanese Life*. Cambridge, MA: MIT Press.

Ito, Mizuko, Sonja Baumer, Matteo Bittanti, danah boyd, Rachel Cody, Becky Herr Stephenson, Heather Horst, et al. (2010) *Hanging Out, Messing Around, and Geeking Out: Kids Living and Learning with New Media*. Cambridge, MA: MIT Press.

Ito, Mizuko, Daisuke Okabe, and Izumi Tsuji, eds (2012) *Fandom Unbound: Otaku Culture in a Connected World*. New Haven, CT: Yale University Press.

Ito, Mizuko, Kris Gutiérrez, Sonia Livingstone, Bill Penuel, Jean Rhodes, Katie Salen, Juliet Schor, Julian Sefton-Green, and S. Craig Watkins (2013) *Connected Learning: An Agenda for Research and Design*. Irvine, CA: Digital Media and Learning Research Hub.

Ito, Mizuko, Elisabeth Soep, Neta Kliger-Vilenchik, Sangita Shresthova, Liana Gamber-Thompson, and Arely Zimmerman (2015) "Learning Connected Civics: Narratives, Practices, and Infrastructures," *Curriculum Inquiry* 45(1): 10–29.

James, Allison, and Alan Prout (1997) *Constructing and Reconstructing Childhood: Contemporary Issues in the Sociological Study of Childhood*. London: Falmer Press.

James, Carrie (2009) *Young People, Ethics, and the New Digital Media: A Synthesis from the GoodPlay Project*. Cambridge: MIT Press/ MacArthur Foundation.

Janissary Collective (2012) "Participatory Culture and Media Life: Approaching Freedom," pp. 257–65 in *The Participatory Cultures Handbook*, ed. Aaron Delwiche and Jennifer Jacobs Henderson. New York: Routledge.

Jenkins, Henry (1992) *Textual Poachers: Television Fans and Participatory Culture*. New York: Routledge.

Jenkins, Henry (2006) *Convergence Culture: Where Old and New Media Collide*. New York: New York University Press.

Jenkins, Henry (2012) "'Cultural Acupuncture': Fan Activism and the Harry Potter Alliance," *Transformative Works and Cultures* 10, http://journal.transformativeworks.org/index.php/twc/article/ view/305/259.

Jenkins, Henry, with Katherine Clinton, Ravi Purushotma, Alice J. Robison, and Margaret Weigel (2007) *Confronting the Challenges of a Participatory Culture: Media Education for the 21st Century*. Chicago: MacArthur Foundation.

Jenkins, Henry, Sam Ford, and Joshua Green (2013) *Spreadable Media: Creating Meaning and Value in a Networked Culture*. New York: New York University Press.

Jenkins, Henry, Erin Reilly, and Ritesh Mehta (2013) *Flows of Reading*. Los Angeles: Annenberg Innovation Lab; http://scalar.usc.edu/ anvc/flowsofreading/index.

Jenkins, Henry, and Wyn Kelley, with Katie Clinton, Jenna McWilliams, Ricardo Pitts-Wiley and Erin Reilly (2013) *Reading in a Participatory*

Culture: Remixing Moby-Dick in the English Classroom. New York: Teachers College Press.

Johnson, Steven (2012) *Future Perfect: The Case for Progress in a Networked Age.* New York: Riverhead.

Kafai, Yasmin, and Michael Resnick, eds ([1996] 2012) *Constructionism in Practice: Designing, Thinking, and Learning in a Digital World.* Mahwah, NJ: Lawrence Erlbaum.

Kligler-Vilenchik, Neta (2013) *"Decreasing World Suck": Fan Communities, Mechanisms of Translation, and Participatory Politics.* University of Southern California, Annenberg School for Communication and Journalism.

Kligler-Vilenchik, Neta, and Sangita Shresthova (2012) *Learning through Practice: Participatory Culture Civics.* University of Southern California, Annenberg School for Communication and Journalism; available at http://dmlcentral.net/sites/dmlcentral/files/resource_files/learning_through_practice_kligler-shresthova_oct-2-2012.pdf.

Kligler-Vilenchik, Neta, Joshua McVeigh-Schultz, Christine Weitbrecht, and Chris Tokuhama (2012) "Experiencing Fan Activism: Understanding the Power of Fan Activist Organizations through Members' Narratives," *Transformative Works and Cultures* 10.

Klink, Flourish (2010) "Verb Noire," in *From Participatory Culture to Public Participation,* https://sites.google.com/site/participatorydemocracyproject/case-studies/verb-noire.

Korobkova, Ksenia (2013) "Will the Real Fan Please Stand Up?" *Connected Learning Research Network Blog,* http://clrn.dmlhub.net/content/will-the-real-fan-please-stand-up.

Kow, Yong Ming, and Bonnie Nardi (2010) "Who Owns the Mods?" *First Monday* 15(5).

Lakhani, Karim R., and Robert G. Wolf (2005) "Why Hackers Do What They Do: Understanding Motivation and Effort in Free/Open Source Software Projects," pp. 3–22 in *Perspectives on Free and Open Source Software,* ed. Joseph Feller, Brian Fitzgerald, Scott Hissam, and Karim R Lakhani. Cambridge, MA: MIT Press.

Lange, Patricia (2014) *Kids on YouTube: Technical Identities and Digital Literacies*. Walnut Creek, CA: Left Coast Press.

Larson, Kiley, Mizuko Ito, Eric Brown, Mike Hawkins, Nichole Pinkard, and Penny Sebring (2013) *Safe Space and Shared Interests: YOUMedia Chicago as a Laboratory for Connected Learning*. Irvine, CA: Digital Media and Learning Research Hub.

Lave, Jean (1988) *Cognition in Practice: Mind, Mathematics and Culture in Everyday Life*. Cambridge: Cambridge University Press.

Lave, Jean (2011) *Apprenticeship in Critical Ethnographic Practice*. Chicago: University of Chicago Press.

Lave, Jean, and Etienne Wenger (1991) *Situated Learning: Legitimate Peripheral Participation*. Cambridge: Cambridge University Press.

Lessig, Lawrence (2004) *Free Culture: The Nature and Future of Creativity*. New York: Penguin.

Lessig, Lawrence (2006) *Code: Version 2.0*. New York: Basic Books.

Levine, Madeline (2006) *The Price of Privilege: How Parental Pressure and Material Advantage Are Creating a Generation of Disconnected and Unhappy Kids*. New York: HarperCollins.

Levy, Nathaniel, Sandra Cortesi, Urs Gasser, Edward Crowley, Meredith Beaton, June Casey, and Caroline Nolan (2012) *Bullying in a Networked Era: A Literature Review*. Berkman Center for Internet & Society at Harvard University, http://cyber.law.harvard.edu/publications/2012/kbw_bulling_in_a_networked_era.

Levy, Pierre (1999) *Collective Intelligence: Mankind's Emerging World in Cyberspace*. New York: Basic Books.

Lipsitz, George (2006) "Learning from New Orleans: The Social Warrant of Hostile Privatism and Competitive Consumer Citizenship," *Cultural Anthropology* 21(3): 451–68.

Livingstone, Sonia (2002) *Young People and New Media*. London: Sage.

Livingstone, Sonia (2009) *Children and the Internet*. Cambridge: Polity.

Livingstone, Sonia, Leslie Haddon, and Anke Gorzig, eds (2012) *Children, Risk and Safety on the Internet: Research and Policy Challenges in Comparative Perspective*. Bristol: Policy Press.

Lotan, Gilad (2012) "KONY2012: See How Invisible Networks

Helped a Campaign Capture the World's Attention," http://giladlotan.com/2012/03/data-viz-kony2012-see-how-invisible-networks-helped-a-campaign-capture-the-worlds-attention/.

Martin, Crystle (2014) *Learning the Ropes: Connected Learning in a WWE Fan Community*. Irvine, CA: Digital Media and Learning Research Hub.

Marwick, Alice (2008) "To Catch a Predator? The MySpace Moral Panic," *First Monday* 13(6), http://firstmonday.org/ojs/index.php/fm/article/view/2152/1966.

Marwick, Alice (2013) *Status Update: Celebrity, Publicity, and Branding in the Social Media Age*. New Haven, CT: Yale University Press.

Marwick, Alice, and danah boyd (2014a) "'It's Just Drama': Teen Perspectives on Conflict and Aggression in a Networked Era," *Journal of Youth Studies* 17(9): 1187–204.

Marwick, Alice, and danah boyd (2014b) "Networked Privacy: How Teenagers Negotiate Context in Social Media," *New Media & Society* 16(7): 1051–67.

Matsuda, Misa (2005) "Mobile Communication and Selective Sociality," pp. 173–94 in *Personal, Portable, Pedestrian: Mobile Phones in Japanese Life*, ed. Mizuko Ito, Misa Matsuda, and Daisuke Okabe. Cambridge, MA: MIT Press.

McDermott, Raymond (1980) "'Let's Try to Make it a Good Day' – Some Not So Simple Ways," *Discourse Processes* 3: 155–68.

McRobbie, Angela (1991) *Feminism and Youth Culture*. London: Routledge.

Meyer, Stephanie (2008) *Twilight*. New York: Little, Brown.

Meyrowitz, Joshua (1985) *No Sense of Place: The Impact of Electronic Media on Social Behavior*. Oxford: Oxford University Press.

Mittell, Jason (2004) *Genre and Television: From Cop Shows to Cartoons in American Culture*. New York: Routledge.

Muggleton, David, and Rupert Weinzierl, eds (2004) *The Post-Subcultures Reader*. London: Bloomsbury.

Nielsen (2010) "African-Americans, Women, and Southerners Talk and Text the Most in the U.S." *Nielsen Newswire*, http://blog.nielsen.

com/nielsenwire/online_mobile/african-americans-women-and-southerners-talk-and-text-the-most-in-the-u-s/.

O'Reilly, Tim (2005) "What Is Web 2.0? Design Patterns and Business Models for the Next Generation of Software," *O'Reilly Media*, http://oreilly.com/web2/archive/what-is-web-20.html.

O'Reilly, Tim, and John Battelle (2009) "Web Squared: Web 2.0 Five Years On," *Web 2.0 Summit*, www.web2summit.com/web2009/public/schedule/detail/10194.

Orr, Julian E. (1996) *Talking about Machines: An Ethnography of a Modern Job*. Ithaca, NY: Cornell University Press.

Papert, Seymour (1975) "Some Poetic and Social Criteria for Education Design," paper presented at the HUMRRO Conference, September 16–18, www.papert.org/articles/SomePoeticAndSocialCriteriaFor EducationDesign.html.

Papert, Seymour (1993) *The Children's Machine: Rethinking School in the Age of the Computer*. New York: Basic Books.

Pariser, Eli (2011) *The Filter Bubble: What the Internet Is Hiding from You*. New York: Penguin.

Pascale, Richard, Jerry Sternin, and Monique Sternin (2010) *The Power of Positive Deviance: How Unlikely Innovators Solve the World's Toughest Problems*. Cambridge, MA: Harvard Business Review Press.

Perkel, Dan (2008) "Copy and Paste Literacy? Literacy Practices in the Production of a MySpace Profile," pp. 203–24 in *Informal Learning and Digital Media: Constructions, Contexts, Consequences*, ed. Kirsten Drotner, Hans Siggaard Jensen, and Kim Christian Schrøder. Newcastle: Cambridge Scholars.

Pope, Denise C. (2001) *Doing School: How We Are Creating a Generation of Stressed Out, Materialistic, and Miseducated Students*. New Haven, CT: Yale University Press.

Rafalow, Matthew H., and Kiley Larson (2014) *Fashioning Learning: Connected Learning through Fashion Design Programs*. Irvine, CA: Digital Media and Learning Research Hub.

Rheingold, Howard (1993) *The Virtual Community: Homesteading on the Electronic Frontier*. New York: Addison Wesley.

Rheingold, Howard (2012) *Net Smart: How to Thrive Online*. Cambridge, MA: MIT Press.

Rideout, Victoria J., Ulla G. Foehr, and Donald R. Roberts (2010) *Generation M2: Media in the Lives of 8- to 18-Year-Olds*. Washington, DC: Kaiser Family Foundation.

Ross, Andrew (1991) *Strange Weather: Culture, Science and Technology in the Age of Limits*. London: Verso.

Rotundo, E. Anthony (1994) *American Manhood: Transformations in Masculinity for the Revolution to the Modern Era*. New York: Basic Books.

Salen, Katie, Robert Torres, Loretta Wolozin, Rebecca Rufo-Tepper, and Arana Shapiro (2011) *Quest to Learn: Developing the School for Digital Kids*. Cambridge, MA: MIT Press.

Savage, Jon (2007) *Teenage: The Creation of Youth Culture*. New York: Viking.

Savchuk, Katia (2011) "Massive Digital Divide for Native Americans Is 'a Travesty,'" *PBS*, www.pbs.org/mediashift/2011/05/massive-digital-divide-for-native-americans-is-a-travesty132/.

Schor, Juliet B., and Craig J. Thompson, eds (2014) *Sustainable Lifestyles and the Quest for Plenitude: Case Studies of the New Economy*. New Haven, CT: Yale University Press.

Schrock, Andrew, and danah boyd (2008) *Online Threats to Youth: Solicitation, Harassment, and Problematic Content*. Berkman Center for Internet & Society at Harvard University.

Seiter, Ellen (1995) *Sold Separately: Children and Parents in Consumer Culture*. New Brunswick, NJ: Rutgers University Press.

Seiter, Ellen (2005) *The Internet Playground: Children's Access, Entertainment, and Mis-Education*. New York: Peter Lang.

Shirky, Clay (2006) "Tiny Slice, Big Market," *Wired* 14(11), www.wired.com/wired/archive/14.11/meganiche.html.

Shresthova, Sangita (2013) *Between Storytelling and Surveillance: American Muslim Youth Negotiate Culture, Politics and Participation*. University of Southern California, Annenberg School for Communication and Journalism.

Springhall, John (1998) *Youth, Popular Culture and Moral Panics*. New York: St Martin's Press.

Stephenson, Catherine L., and Becky Herr Belcher (2013) *Teaching Harry Potter*. New York: Palgrave Macmillan.

Stone, Linda (n.d.) Continuous Partial Attention, http://lindastone.net/qa/continuous-partial-attention/.

Suchman, Lucy A. (1987) *Plans and Situated Actions: The Problem of Human–Machine Communication*. Cambridge: Cambridge University Press.

Sunstein, Cass R. (2009) *Republic.com 2.0*. Princeton, NJ: Princeton University Press.

Swartz, Aaron (2006) "Who Writes Wikipedia?," *Wikimedia 2006 Elections*, www.aaronsw.com/weblog/whowriteswikipedia.

Tamagawa, Hiroaki (2012) "Comic Market as a Space for Self-Expression in Otaku Culture," pp. 107–32 in *Fandom Unbound: Otaku Culture in a Connected World*, ed. Mizuko Ito, Daisuke Okabe, and Izumi Tsuji. New Haven, CT: Yale University Press.

Terranova, Tiziana (2003) "Free Labor: Producing Culture for the Digital Economy," *Electronic Book Review*, June 20, www.electronicbookreview.com/thread/technocapitalism/voluntary.

Tulloch, John, and Henry Jenkins (1995) *Science Fiction Audiences: Watching "Doctor Who" and "Star Trek."* London: Routledge.

Valentine, Gill (2004) *Public Space and the Culture of Childhood*. Aldershot: Ashgate.

Varnelis, Kazys, ed. (2008) *Networked Publics*. Cambridge, MA: MIT Press.

Warner, Michael (2002) *Publics and Counterpublics*. Cambridge, MA: Zone Books.

Watkins, S. Craig (2010) *The Young and the Digital: What the Migration to Social Network Sites, Games, and Anytime, Anywhere Media Means for the Future*. Boston: Beacon Press.

Weber, Steven (2005) *The Success of Open Source*. Cambridge, MA: Harvard University Press.

Wellman, Barry (1999) *Networks in the Global Village: Life in Contemporary Communities.* Boulder, CO: Westview Press.

Williams, Raymond (1958) "Culture Is Ordinary," pp. 91–100 in *The Everyday Life Reader*, ed. Ben Highmore. London: Routledge.

Willis, Paul (1981) *Learning to Labor: How Working Class Kids Get Working Class Jobs.* New York: Columbia University Press.

Zickuhr, Kathryn, and Aaron Smith (2012) *Digital Differences.* Pew Internet & American Life Project, 13.

Zimmerman, Arely (2012) *Documenting DREAMs: New Media, Undocumented Youth and the Immigrant Rights Movement.* Los Angeles: Media Activism and Participatory Politics.

Zittrain, Jonathan (2008) *The Future of the Internet – and How to Stop it.* New Haven, CT: Yale University Press.

Zuckerman, Ethan (2013) "Beyond the Crisis in Civics," talk given at the Digital Media and Learning Conference, Chicago, March 14–16, http://dml2013.dmlhub.net/content/videos-day-1-keynote-ignite-talks.

Zuckerman, Ethan (2014) "A Public Apology – on Screwing Up by Not Questioning Assumptions – my talk at #BIF10," www.ethan-zuckerman.com/blog/2014/09/17/a-public-apology-on-scr ewing-up-by-not-questioning-assumptions-my-talk-at-bif10/.

Index